York St John College
Fountains Learning Cen

Footprints On The Page

Poetry Collection 1

Published by Evans Brothers Limited
2A Portman Mansions
Chiltern Street
London W1U 6NR

First published in 1998
Reprinted in 2000
First published in paperback in 2001

Printed in Scotland by Omnia Books Limited, Glasgow

Editor: Su Swallow
Design: Neil Sayer
Production: Jenny Mulvanny

British Library Cataloguing in Publication Data
Footprints on the Page: Poety Collection 1
1.Children's poetry
I.Waters, Fiona
808.8'1

ISBN 0237523418

Dedication

For Stephen Heffer, much missed friend.

ACKNOWLEDGEMENTS

Background image Alan Towse **page 10, 12** Adam Woolfitt/Robert Harding Picture Library **page 14** Andrew Sanders/Robert Harding Picture Library **page 16** Mark Mawson/Robert Harding Picture Library **page 20, 23, 27** Robert Harding Picture Library **page 28** Michael Freeman/Bruce Coleman Limited **page 33, 35** Last Resort Picture Library **page 37, 44** Robert Harding Picture Library **page 45, 49, 54, 56-57, 59, 63** Last Resort Picture Library **page 64** Robert Harding Picture Library **page 67** Last Resort Picture Library **page 75** R Scagell/Robert Harding Picture Library **page 77** Jane Burton/Bruce Coleman Limited **page 80, 83** Last Resort Picture Library **page 100** Ake Sandstrom/Robert Harding Picture Library **page 107** Andrew J Purcell/Bruce Coleman Limited **page 108** Julie Habe/Robert Harding Picture Library **page 110** Tan Griffiths/Robert Harding Picture Library **page 113** Robert Harding Picture Library **page 115** Staffan Widstrand/Bruce Coleman Limited **page 117** Len Rue Jr/Bruce Coleman Limited **page 122** Robert Harding Picture Library **page 125** Ian Griffiths/Robert Harding Picture Library **page 129** Louise Murray/Robert Harding Picture Library **page 130/131** Robert Harding Picture Library **page 136** Roy Rainford/Robert Harding Picture Library **page 141** Robert Harding Picture Library **page 152** Robin Scagell/Robert Harding Picture Library **page 155** S Villeger/Explorer/Robert Harding Picture Library

Footprints On The Page

Poetry Collection 1

Compiled by
Fiona Waters

Evans Brothers Limited

CONTENTS

The Seasons, Country Life

My New Year's Resolutions *Robert Fisher* 9
The Months *Sara Coleridge* 10
The Weather *Gavin Ewart* 11
Chinese New Year *Wendy Larmont* 12
At Long Last, Spring Has Arrived!
    Colin McNaughton 13
A Change in the Year
    William Wordsworth 13
Time to Dust the Daffodils *Irene Rawnsley* 14
Summer Days *Bital Patel* 15
Rain in Summer
    Henry Wadsworth Longfellow 16
Windy Nights *Robert Louis Stevenson* 16
The Biggest Firework *Anon* 17
The Fog *FR McCreary* 18
Wind Poem *Pie Corbett* 18
Snow Clouds *Daphne Lister* 19

City Life, Homes

Concrete Mixers *Patricia Hubbell* 20
Out in the City *Gareth Owen* 21
Graffiti *Joan Poulson* 22
Looking Down on Roofs *Marian Lines* 24
The Wraggle Taggle Gipsies *Trad* 24
If I Moved House *Nicola Brophy* 26

Sounds

The Electronic House *Wes Magee* 26
Washing up *Sarah Gunn* 28
Underwater, Holding Nose *Jez Alborough* 29
The Sound Collector *Roger McGough* 30

Food

Give Up Slimming Mum *Kit Wright* 32
Mango *Grace Nichols* 33

A Lesson *Brian Morse* 34
Breakfast *Danielle Sensier* 34
I'd Like to be a Teabag *Peter Dixon* 36
Mushrooms *Berlie Doherty* 37
I Had a Nickel *Anonymous* 38
Chips *Stanley Cook* 38
Opening a Packet of Biscuits *Pat Moon* 39
Ten Fat Sausages *Anon* 40

School

The Marrog *R.C. Scriven* 41
The Dragon Who Ate Our School
    Nick Toczek 42
The Pocket Calculator *Stanley Cook* 44
Mystery Story *Eric Finney* 45

Music, Words

Break Dance *Grace Nichols* 46
Kitchen Noises *Matthew Hinton* 47
My Bargain Bag of Question Marks
    Barry Buckingham 48
Thumping, Stumping, Bumping, Jumping
    Anon 49
Hints on Pronunciation *Anon* 50
The Young Bard of Japan *Anon* 50
Learning to Read *Daniel Ribenfors* 51
Music *Tony Mitton* 52
Words I Like *Steve Turner* 53

Hands, Knees...

Hands *Peter Young* 54
Hair *Aaron Lockwood* 54
Knees *Katie Wilson* 55
Jamaican Clap Rhyme *Anon* 55
Socks *Colin West* 56

Numbers

One Old Ox *Anon* **58**
The Surprising Number 37 *Anon* **58**
Two Times Table *Anon* **59**
The Dream of a Boy Who Lived at Nine Elms
 William Brighty Rands **60**
Twelve Huntsmen *Anon* **61**

Colours

I asked the Little Boy Who Cannot See
 Anon **62**
What is Black? *Mary O'Neil* **62**
What is Pink? *Christina Rossetti* **64**
The Paint Box *EV Rieu* **64**
Today in Strong Colours *Sue Cowling* **65**

Secrets

Little Brother's Secret
 Katherine Mansfield **66**
The Secret Brother *Elizabeth Jennings* **66**
The Secret Place *Tomie de Paola* **68**
Jealousy *Terry Baylis* **69**
Pearls *Jean Little* **69**
Treasure Trove *Irene Rawnsley* **70**

Ghosts

Walls I Scream *Philip C Gross* **72**
Voice in the Night *Joan Poulson* **74**
I Like to Stay Up *Grace Nichols* **76**

Witches and Magic

The Witch's Cat *Ian Serrailler* **77**
The Hairy Toe *Trad* **78**
The Witch and the AA Man
 Barry Buckingham **80**
Queen Nerfertiti *Anon* **82**
The Speller's Bag *John Agard* **83**
The Sleepy Giant *Charles E Carryl* **84**

A Spell for Sleeping *Alastair Reid* **84**

Thoughts

Whoppers *Eric Finney* **86**
Unemployable *Gareth Owen* **87**
It's Raining Cats and Dogs *Steve Turner* **87**
I've Never Heard the Queen Sneeze
 Brian Patten **88**
Wanted *Michael Harrison* **89**
St George and the Dragon *Finola Akister* **90**

Nonsense

Fisherman's Tale *Irene Rawnsley* **91**
Imagine *Anon* **92**
Queer Things *James Reeves* **93**
The Spangled Pandemonium
 Palmer Brown **94**
A Tragic Story
 William Makepeace Thackeray **95**
The Relentless Pursuit of the 12-toed
 Snortibog *Anon* **96**
When Fishes Set Umbrellas Up
 Christina Rossetti **96**
The Quangle Wangle's Hat *Edward Lear* **97**

Cats...

Guardian *Keith Bosley* **99**
Sleeping Cats *Moira Andrew* **100**
The Cats of Kilkenny *Anon* **101**
My Cat *Nigel Gray* **102**

...and Dogs

Bumblefoot *Colin Thiele* **103**
Roger the Dog *Ted Hughes* **104**
Burying the Dog in the Garden
 Brian Patten **105**

Animals and Birds

Mare *Judith Thurman* 106
The Frog *Anon* 107
Blue Tits *Geoffrey Holloway* 107
The Hen *Lord Alfred Douglas* 108
The Heron *Gregory Harrison* 109
Life as a Sheep *Gareth Owen* 110
Anne and the Field Mouse *Ian Serraillier* 112
First Fox *Pamela Gillilan* 113
Fable *Ralph Waldo Emerson* 114
The Bat *Theodore Roethke* 114
Camel *Mary Britton Miller* 115
The Pyramids *Mike Jubb* 116
If You Should Meet a Crocodile *Anon* 116
Geraldine Giraffe *Colin West* 117
The Parrot *Thomas Campbell* 118
Two Octopuses Got Married
    Remy Charlip 119
Who Will Go First? *Kevin Horton* 120
Chameleons *Colin West* 120

The Sea

Spring Fjord *Traditional Inuit Song* 121
The Lighthouse *Raymond Wilson* 122
Coral *Christina Rossetti* 122
That Sinking Feeling *Anon* 123
The Monster *Jean Kenward* 124
Sea Timeless Song *Grace Nichols* 125
How to Make a Sailor's Pie *Joan Aiken* 126
Old Man Ocean *Russell Hoban* 126

Conservation

The Walk *Michelle Walker* 127
Goliath *Spike Milligan* 127
Mummy, Oh Mummy *Anon* 128
Tiger in a Zoo *Pat Moon* 129
An Alphabet for the Planet
    Riad Nourallah 130
How Can One Sell the Air? *Chief Seattle* 132

Travel

Real Life *Gareth Owen* 133
Goodbye Granny *Pauline Stewart* 134
A Trip to Morrow *Anon* 135
Overtaking *Ian Larmont* 136
Are We Nearly There Yet? *Lucie Davis* 136
If Only I Could Drive a Train
    Richard Edwards 137
From a Railway Carriage
    Robert Louis Stevenson 138

Families

Seeing All My Family *Claire Salama* 139
Weasles *John Latham* 140
Angry *Donna Fisher* 141
Listn Big Brodda Dread, Na! *James Berry* 142
I Remember My Dad
    Louise Victoria Coce 143
Hands *Tamasyn Sear* 144
There Are Four Chairs Round the Table
    John Foster 144
Firsts *Zoe Gardner* 145
The Wrong Side *Brian Moses* 146
Tea with Aunty Mabel *Jeanne Willis* 146
My Auntie *Colin West* 147
My Granny is a Sumo Wrestler
    Gareth Owen 148
When I am Old *Amelia Clarke* 150

Sleeping and Dreaming

The Sleeping Bag
    Herbert George Ponting 151
Night Lights *Anon* 151
Night Ride *Celia Warren* 152
Grandpa Bear's Lullaby *Jane Yolen* 153
How Far? *Olive Dove* 154
When I Close My Eyes *Andrew Collett* 155

MY NEW YEAR'S RESOLUTIONS

I will not throw the cat out the window
Or put a frog in my sister's bed
I will not tie my brother's shoelaces together
Nor jump from the roof of Dad's shed.
I shall remember my aunt's next birthday
And tidy my room once a week
I'll not moan at Mum's cooking (Ugh! Fish fingers again!)
Nor give her any more of my cheek.
I will not pick my nose if I can help it
I shall fold up my clothes, comb my hair,
I will say please and thank you (even when I don't mean it)
And never spit or shout or even swear.
I shall write each day in my diary
Try my hardest to be helpful at school
I shall help old ladies cross the roads (even if they don't want to)
And when others are rude I'll stay cool.
I'll go to bed with the owls and be up with the larks
And close every door behind me
I shall squeeze from the bottom of every toothpaste tube
And stay where trouble can't find me.
I shall start again, turn over a new leaf,
Leave my bad old ways forever
Shall I start them this year, or next year
Shall I sometime, or ..... ?

Robert Fisher

THE MONTHS

January brings the snow,
Makes our feet and fingers glow.

February brings the rain,
Thaws the frozen lake again.

March brings breezes loud and shrill,
Stirs the dancing daffodil.

April brings the primrose sweet,
Scatters daisies at our feet.

May brings flocks of pretty lambs,
Skipping by their fleecy dams.

June brings tulips, lilies, roses,
Fills the children's hands with posies.

Hot July brings cooling showers,
Apricots and gillyflowers.

August brings the sheaves of corn,
Then the harvest home is borne.

Warm September brings the fruit,
Sportsmen then begin to shoot.

Fresh October brings the pheasant,
Then to gather nuts is pleasant.

Dull November brings the blast,
Then the leaves are whirling fast.

Chill December brings the sleet,
Blazing fire, and Christmas treat.

Sara Coleridge

THE WEATHER

What's the weather on about?
Why is the rain so down on us?
Why does the sun glare at us so?

Why does the hail dance so prettily?
Why is the snow such an overall?
Why is the wind such a tearaway?

Why is the mud so fond of our feet?
Why is the ice so keen to upset us?
Who does the weather think it is?

Gavin Ewart

CHINESE NEW YEAR

Dragons, lions,
Red and gold.
In with the New Year,
Out with the old.

Banners flying,
Bands playing.
Lion prancing,
Dragon swaying.

Fireworks cracking,
Lanterns swinging,
People laughing,
Dancing, singing.

Dragons, lions,
Red and gold.
In with the New Year,
Out with the Old.

Wendy Larmont

AT LONG LAST, SPRING HAS ARRIVED!

At long last, spring has arrived.
'So there you are!' I said icily.
'About time too!' I said frostily.
'You're late!' I said coldly.

'Cool it,' she said mildly.
'I've been under a lot of pressure lately.
Have a daffodil.'

'Blooming cheek,' I said,
In the heat of the moment.

Colin McNaughton

A CHANGE IN THE YEAR

It is the first mild day in March:
    Each minute sweeter than before,
The redbreast sings from the tall larch
    That stands beside our door.

There is a blessing in the air,
    Which seems a sense of joy to yield
To the bare trees, and mountain bare,
    And grass in the green field.

William Wordsworth

TIME TO DUST THE DAFFODILS

My gran's too old
to go out
in the cold garden
planting bulbs,
but she likes
spring flowers.

She has a box
of plastic daffodils
on sticks
that she hides away
in the winter.

When she notices
that spring is coming
she takes them out,
dusts each one carefully,

then plants them
underneath her window.

Passers-by pause
to admire them.
'How lovely, Mrs. Paradine!
Why do your daffodils
always bloom earlier
than mine?'

Irene Rawnsley

SUMMER DAYS

Sun's hot
Feet are blazing,
Shoes are sticking
Feel like lazing.

Faces sweating
Hot all round
Cool drinks
There I found.

In the garden
People sitting
Kids running
Grans knitting.

Summer days
Are really nice
Hot days -
Bring some ice.

Bital Patel (Aged 13)

RAIN IN SUMMER

How beautiful is the rain!
After the dust and heat,
In the broad and fiery street,
In the narrow lane,
How beautiful is the rain!
How it clatters along the roofs,
Like the tramp of hoofs!

How it gushes and struggles out
From the throat of the overflowing spout!
Across the window pane
It pours and pours;
And swift and wide,
With a muddy tide,
Like a river down the gutter roars
The rain, the welcome rain!

Henry Wadsworth Longfellow

WINDY NIGHTS

Whenever the moon and
stars are set,
Whenever the wind is high,
All night long in the dark
and wet,
A man goes riding by.
Late in the night when the fires
are out,
Why does he gallop and gallop
about?

Whenever the trees are crying aloud,
    And ships are tossed at sea,
By, on the highway, low and loud,
    By at the gallop goes he;
By at the gallop he goes, and then
By he comes back at the gallop again.

Robert Louis Stevenson

THE BIGGEST FIREWORK

The biggest firework
Ever lit,
Fizzed, banged,
Glittered, flew
In Golden-Silver-
Red-Green-Blue.
It rocketed
So far away,
It brought to night
A burst of day,
Electric bulbs
A million bright
Of shining spray.

But of its fiery magic spell
All that is left
Is the smoke smell ...

Anonymous

THE FOG

Slowly, the fog,
Hunch-shouldered with a grey face,
Arms wide, advances,
Finger-tips touching the way
Past the dark houses
And dark gardens of roses.
Up the short street from the harbour,
Slowly the fog,
Seeking, seeking;
Arms wide, shoulders hunched,
Searching, searching.
Out through the streets to the fields,
Slowly, the fog -
A blind man hunting the moon.

F.R. McCreary

WIND POEM

Wind slices its icy blade.

Wind raids trees,
smacks leaves up back streets.

Wind somersaults sheets,
bustles and kicks.

Wind flexes muscles,
flicks its quivering wrist.

Wind twists dustbins
into clattering cartwheels.

Wind curls its steel tongue
like a shout flung at the sky.

Wind sighs;
Dies.

Pie Corbett

SNOW CLOUDS

Like sulky polar bears
Clouds prowl across the winter sky
From cold and snowy northern lands
As though from icy lairs.

Soon snow begins to fall
Small snippets of the whitest fur
And like the stealthy polar bear
It makes no sound at all.

Daphne Lister

CONCRETE MIXERS

The drivers are washing the concrete mixers;
Like elephant tenders they hose them down.
Tough grey-skinned monsters standing ponderous,
Elephant-bellied and elephant-nosed,
Standing in muck up to their wheel-caps,
Like rows of elephants, tail to trunk.
Their drivers perch on their backs like mahouts,
Sending the sprays of water up.
They rid the trunk-like trough of concrete,
Direct the spray to the bulging sides,
Turn and start the monsters moving.
    Concrete mixers
    Move like elephants
    Bellow like elephants
    Spray like elephants,
Concrete mixers are urban elephants,
Their trunks are raising a city.

Patricia Hubbell

OUT IN THE CITY

When you're out in the city
Shuffling down the street,
A bouncy city rhythm
Starts to boogie in your feet.

It jumps off the pavement,
There's a snare drum in your brain,
It pumps through your heart
Like a diesel train.

There's Harry on the corner,
Sings, 'How she goin' boy?'
To loose and easy Winston
With his brother Leroy.

Shout, 'Hello!' to Bill Brisket
With his tripes and cows heels,
Blood-stained rabbits
And trays of live eels.

Maltese Tony
Smoking in the shade
Keeping one good eye
On the amusement arcade.

Move along
Step this way
Here's a bargain
What you say?
Mind your backs
Here's your stop
More fares?
Room on top.

Neon lights and take-aways
Gangs of girls and boys
Football crowds and market stalls
Taxi cabs and noise.

From the city cafes
On the smoky breeze
Smells of Indian cooking
Greek and Cantonese.

Well, some people like suburban life
Some people like the sea
Others like the countryside
But it's the city
Yes it's the city
It's the city life
For me.

Gareth Owen

GRAFFITI

Over the tracks
back of the flats
it's growing
like a garden.

Round the streets
all concrete
no grass, no trees
nothing green

but

over the tracks
back of the flats
it's growing
like a garden.

There's every colour
you can think of
every shape
every size

words spark
like fire-works
jazzy, dazzling -
mind your eyes.

Zig-Zag letters
fizzle and fall,
squiggles, splodges
surprising the wall.

Spiralling showers
luminous, bright,
fluorescent flowers
fresh overnight.

Over the tracks back of the flats
it's growing
like a garden.

Joan Poulson

LOOKING DOWN ON ROOFS

When I lived in a basement,
The house above my head
Was like a mountain of brick and wood,
A place of weight and dread.
But now I'm in a Tower Block
I can look right down my nose
At the mingy, stingy streets below,
That lie beneath my toes.

When I lived in a basement,
I smelled the damp all night;
And the cats and rats of the neighbourhood
Would choose our yard to fight.
But now I'm in a Tower Block,
It's clean, and fresh, and high, -
And I love to look down on the roofs and know
That I'm nearer to the sky.

Marian Lines

THE WRAGGLE TAGGLE GIPSIES

There were three gipsies a-come to my door,
And down-stairs ran this a-lady, O!
One sang high, and another sang low,
And the other sang, Bonny, bonny Biscay, O!

Then she pulled off her silk-finished gown
And put on hose of leather, O!
The ragged, ragged rags about our door -
She's gone with the wraggle taggle gipsies, O!

It was late last night, when my lord came home,
Enquiring for his a-lady, O!
The servants said, on every hand:
'She's gone with the wraggle taggle gipsies, O!'

'O saddle to me my milk-white steed,
Go and fetch me my pony, O!
That I may ride and seek my bride,
Who is gone with the wraggle taggle gipsies, O!'

O he rode high and he rode low,
He rode through woods and copses too,
Until he came to an open field,
And there he espied his a-lady, O!

'What makes you leave your house and land?
What makes you leave your money, O?
What makes you leave your new-wedded lord;
To go with the wraggle taggle gipsies, O!'

'What care I for my house and my land?
What care I for my money, O?
What care I for my new-wedded lord?
I'm off with the wraggle taggle gipsies, O!'

'Last night you slept on a goose-feather bed,
With the sheet turned down so bravely, O!
And to-night you'll sleep in a cold open field,
Along with the wraggle taggle gipsies, O!'

'What care I for a goose-feather bed,
With the sheet turned down so bravely, O?
For to-night I shall sleep in a cold open field,
Along with the wraggle taggle gipsies, O!'

Traditional

IF I MOVED HOUSE!

If I moved house I'd take:
The times we canoe in the field when it floods,
my gerbil's grave
and the sound of the stream.

I wouldn't take:
the cat next door,
or the man next door.
They make noises in the night.

I'd take:
The mossy greenhouse
and the helicopter seeds,
the sheep making noises behind the house
and the sycamore tree I climb in.

I wouldn't take:
The smoke from next door when she has a fire.
Or the alarm that goes off when Mum burns the cooking.

But I would take:
The weeping willow that hangs over the stream.

Nicola Brophy (Aged 10)

THE ELECTRONIC HOUSE

cooker. blanket.
toothbrush. fire.
iron. light-bulb.
tv. drier.

fridge. radio.
robot. drill.
crimper. speaker.
kettle. grill.
slicer. grinder.
meters. fan.
slide-projector.
deep-fry pan.
vacuum-cleaner.
fuses. shocks.
freezer. shaver.
junction box.
water heater.
Christmas lamps.
knife. recorder.
cables. amps.
door chimes. organ.
infra red.
guitar. video.
sunlamp bed.
synthesizer.
night light glow.
cultivator.
stereo.
calculator.
metronome.
toaster. teasmade!
ohm, sweet, ohm.

Wes Magee

WASHING UP

Soapy Bubbles that squelch and squirm
A big bowl of water, wet and warm
Squeaky dishes that slide and slip
It's not so bad when you get into it!

With sleeves rolled up and bubbles galore
A rainbow wonderland in every tiny mirror ball
Reflecting a hundred matching faces
Shiny tea cups, silver spoons and empty spaces.

If you cup your hands and blow them high
Into the air they'll dance and fly
Until the glistening pops and silently disappears
Leaving fingers wrinkled soft and wet, and then,
'Are those dishes all washed up yet?'

Sarah Gunn (Aged 10)

UNDERWATER, HOLDING NOSE

Underwater, holding nose,
     dive,
        dive,
    down he goes.
Eerie noises, heartbeat beating,
     water pipes
  and central heating.
Gliding forward, no one knows,
  Along the slimy bath he goes.

  Distant voices,
   bubbles rise,
    stinging water, screwed up eyes.
Cheeks are bulging, pressure grows.
  Wrinkled fingers,
  crinkled toes.
  Surface quickly,
  come up clean ...
He's the human submarine.

Jez Alborough

THE SOUND COLLECTOR

A stranger called this morning
Dressed all in black and grey
Put every sound into a bag
And carried them away

The whistling of the kettle
The turning of the lock
The purring of the kitten
The ticking of the clock

The popping of the toaster
The crunching of the flakes
When you spread the marmalade
The scraping noise it makes

The hissing of the frying-pan
The ticking of the grill
The bubbling of the bathtub
As it starts to fill

The drumming of the raindrops
On the window-pane
When you do the washing-up
The gurgle of the drain

The crying of the baby
The squeaking of the chair
The swishing of the curtain
The creaking of the stair

A stranger called this morning
He didn't leave his name
Left us only silence
Life will never be the same.

Roger McGough

GIVE UP SLIMMING, MUM

My Mum
is short
and plump
and pretty
and I wish
she'd give up
slimming.

So does Dad.

Her cooking's
delicious -
you can't
beat it -
but you really can
hardly bear
to eat it -
the way she sits
with her eyes
brimming,
watching you
polish off
the spuds
and trimmings
while she
has nothing
herself but a small
thin dry
diet biscuit:
that's all

My Mum
is short

and plump
and pretty
and I wish
she'd give up
slimming.

So does Dad.

She says she
looks as though
someone had
sat on her -
BUT WE LIKE MUM
WITH A BIT
OF FAT ON HER!

Kit Wright

MANGO

Have a mango
sweet rainwashed sunripe
mango
that the birds themselves
woulda pick
if only they had seen it
a rosy miracle

Here
take it from mih hand

Grace Nichols

A LESSON

Darren took all
the labels off
the tins in Mummy's
shopping bag.

He sorted them
like teacher had,
red and yellow,
green and blue.

Tonight the dog
had soup for tea,
the cat had beans
and Darren had

Whiskas.
He said it
tasted horrible
on toast.

Brian Morse

BREAKFAST

Mum makes me eat muesli.
I always try a 'no' but

    she just says
    it's good for me to
    eat a bowl of
    oats and bran that's

full of fruit, nutritious nuts and
vitamins B, C and D.

It helps your insides go.

Mum makes Dad eat muesli.
He always pulls a face but

she just says
it's good for him he's
overweight and
not that young and
ought to think about his heart and
throw away the frying pan.

You'll get used to the taste.

This morning very early before the world was up,
strange sounds from the kitchen
something sizzling, something hot.

So I
crept down
quick and quiet
on ten tip-toes to
find out

Who was secretively scoffing
eggs and bacon?

It was Mum!

Danielle Sensier

I'D LIKE TO BE A TEABAG

I'd like to be a teabag,
And stay at home all day -
And talk to other teabags
In a teabag sort of way …

I'd love to be a teabag,
And lie in a little box -
And never have to wash my face
Or change my dirty socks …

I'd like to be a teabag,
An Earl Grey one perhaps,
And doze all day and lie around
With Earl Grey kind of chaps.

I wouldn't have to do a thing,
No homework, jobs or chores -
Comfy in my caddy
Of teabags and their snores.

I wouldn't have to do exams,
I needn't tidy rooms,
Or sweep the floor or feed the cat
Or wash up all the spoons.

I wouldn't have to do a thing,
A life of bliss - you see …
Except that once in all my life

I'd make a cup of tea!

Peter Dixon

MUSHROOMS

Bald things,
Thrust heads through soil
And commune
Pale and quiet
In their own damp smell.

Their stems pop when they're plucked
Their skin peels away
Their peat-cool flesh is soft.

Fried in hot butter
They grow plump as the slugs
That slithered round their stems,
They gleam with oozed sweat.

And when they're bitten
They burst
Spilling juices
That taste of grass
And fresh dew trodden in by horses
And foxy woodland
And the deep moist brown dark earth.

Berlie Doherty

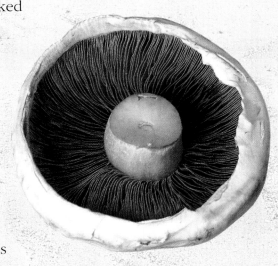

I HAD A NICKEL

I had a nickel and I walked around the block.
I walked right into a baker shop.
I took two doughnuts right out of the grease;
I handed the lady my five-cent piece.
She looked at the nickel and she looked at me,
And said, 'This money's no good to me.
There's a hole in the nickel, and it goes right through.'
Says I, 'There's a hole in the doughnut, too.'

Anonymous

CHIPS

Out of the paper bag
Comes the hot breath of the chips
And I shall blow on them
To stop them burning my lips.

Before I leave the counter
The woman shakes
Raindrops of vinegar on them
And salty snowflakes.

Outside the frosty pavements
Are slippery as a slide
But the chips and I
Are warm inside.

Stanley Cook

OPENING A PACKET OF BISCUITS

She pulled the tab that says TEAR HERE
But alas, the tab tore clear.
She tried to peel the sealed end-flaps
But nothing could prise back those wraps.
What could she do to extract
Those biscuits so inscrutably wrapped?
She took a knife and attacked it,
Sawed and slashed, stabbed and hacked it.
Really thought that she had cracked it
Till she surveyed the stubborn packet.
From the wraps so tightly sealed
At last the biscuits were revealed,
But her plan had not succeeded,
"Oh crumbs," she said,
"That's all I needed."

_____

Pat Moon

TEN FAT SAUSAGES

Ten fat sausages frying in the pan,
Ten fat sausages frying in the pan,
One went POP and another went BANG!
Then there were eight fat sausages frying in the pan.

Eight fat sausages frying in the pan,
Eight fat sausages frying in the pan,
One went POP and another went BANG!
Then there were six fat sausages frying in the pan.

Six fat sausages frying in the pan,
Six fat sausages frying in the pan,
One went POP and another went BANG!
Then there were four fat sausages frying in the pan.

Four fat sausages frying in the pan,
Four fat sausages frying in the pan,
One went POP and another went BANG!
Then there were two fat sausages frying in the pan.

Two fat sausages frying in the pan,
Two fat sausages frying in the pan,
One went POP and another went BANG!
Then there were no fat sausages frying in the pan!

Anonymous

THE MARROG

My desk's at the back of the class
    And nobody, nobody knows
        I'm a Marrog from Mars
With a body of brass
    And seventeen fingers and toes.

Wouldn't they shriek if they knew
    I've three eyes at the back of my head
        And my hair is bright purple
My nose is deep blue
    And my teeth are half-yellow, half-red.

My five arms are silver, and spiked
    With knives on them sharper than spears.
I could go back right now, if I liked -
    And return in a million light-years.

I could gobble them all,
For I'm seven foot tall
    And I'm breathing green flames from my ears.

Wouldn't they yell if they knew,
    If they guessed that a Marrog was here?
Ha-ha, they haven't a clue -
    Or wouldn't they tremble with fear!
'Look, look, a Marrog'
    They'd all scream - and SMACK
The blackboard would fall and the ceiling would crack
    And teacher would faint, I suppose.
But I grin to myself, sitting right at the back
    And nobody, nobody knows.

R. C. Scriven

THE DRAGON
WHO ATE OUR SCHOOL

The day the dragon came to call,
she ate the gate, the playground wall
and, slate by slate, the roof and all,
the staffroom, gym, and entrance hall,
and every classroom, big or small.

So ...
She's undeniably great.
She's absolutely cool,
the dragon who ate
the dragon who ate
the dragon who ate our school.

Pupils panicked. Teachers ran.
She flew at them with wide wingspan.
She slew a few and then began
to chew through the lollipop man,
two parked cars and a transit van.

Wow ... !
She's undeniably great.
She's absolutely cool,
the dragon who ate
the dragon who ate
the dragon who ate our school.

She bit off the head of the head.
She said she was sad he was dead.
He bled and he bled and he bled.
And as she fed, her chin went red
and then she swallowed the cycle shed.

Oh ...
She's undeniably great.
She's absolutely cool,
the dragon who ate
the dragon who ate
the dragon who ate our school.

It's thanks to her that we've been freed.
We needn't write. We needn't read.
Me and my mates are all agreed,
we're very pleased with her indeed.
So clear the way, let her proceed.

Cos ...
She's undeniably great.
She's absolutely cool,
the dragon who ate
the dragon who ate
the dragon who ate our school.

There was some stuff she couldn't eat.
A monster forced to face defeat,
she spat it out along the street -
the dinner ladies' veg and meat
and that pink muck they serve for sweet.

But ...
She's undeniably great.
She's absolutely cool,
the dragon who ate
the dragon who ate
the dragon who ate our school.

Nick Toczek

THE POCKET CALCULATOR

Ready to go to work
The moment it sees the light,
The pocket calculator
Clears its memory
At a touch
And in the panel a nought
Comes out as a flower
Opens to the sun.

Of course, it's always right.
Whether it adds,
subtracts
or multiplies,
Or copies the mistakes I make.
But somehow it seems strange
That whether you lose or gain
Ninety-nine million,
Nine hundred and ninety-nine thousand,
Nine hundred and ninety-nine
Of pounds
Or anything
Its straightfaced look
Will never change.

Stanley Cook

MYSTERY STORY

A morning in May,
And we rolled up to school
In the usual way.

Well no, we didn't really,
Because the school wasn't there;
We rolled up to where
The school had been.
There was nothing.
It had all gone
And there wasn't a clue:
No hole, no scar,
Just a buttercup field
And a couple of larks
Singing over it.

You'd have thought there might be
A lot of cheering from the kids,
But there wasn't.
They all just stood around
Wondering,
Not even talking much.

Eric Finney

BREAK DANCE

I'm going to break dance
turn rippling glass
stretch my muscles
to the bass

Whoo!

I'm going to break dance
I'm going to rip it
and jerk it
and take it apart

I'm going to chop it
and move it
and groove it

Ooooh I'm going to ooze it
electric boogaloo
electric boogaloo
across your floor

I'm going to break dance
watch my ass
take the shine
off your laugh

Whoo!

I'm going to dip it
and spin it
let my spine twist it
I'm going to shift it

and stride it
let my mind glide it

Then I'm going to ease it
ease it
and bring it all home
all home
                 believing in the beat
                 believing in the beat
                 of myself

Grace Nichols

KITCHEN NOISES

Pots and pans bashing
Plates go crashing.
Oven is humming
While washing is drumming.
Taps dripping, scissors snipping.
Cupboards banging
Kitchen door slamming.
Sink gushing
Potato mashing.
Kettle singing
Spoon clinking.
But the thing I like most, even more than toast,
IS …
                Mum's bolognaise.

Matthew Hinton (Aged 6)

MY BARGAIN BAG
OF QUESTION MARKS

I've bought a bag of question marks -
they'd been reduced in price.
The dots look rather boring,
but the curly bits are nice.

However, now I've got them,
what's the next thing I should do?
Are they good for hanging coats on?
Should I put up one or two?

Are they better, though, as egg-whisks?
Or as artificial curls?
Could I make them into earrings
for some very trendy girls?

Should I keep them for the Christmas tree?
Or hang them round a lamp?
Would they go all straight, or wrinkly,
if I ever got them damp?

Are they suitable for fishing?
Or to use as curtain hooks?
If I stuck one on my forehead
would I get some funny looks?

But wait!
The bag is empty.
What a foolish thing I've done!
I've asked too many questions,
and I've used up every one.

Barry Buckingham

THUMPING, STUMPING, BUMPING, JUMPING

Thumping, stumping, bumping, jumping,
Ripping, nipping, tripping, skipping,
All the way home.

Popping, clopping, stopping, hopping,
Stalking, chalking, talking, walking,
All the way home.

Anonymous

HINTS ON PRONUNCIATION

I take it you already know
Of tough and bough and cough and dough?
Others may stumble but not you,
On hiccough, thorough, lough and through?
Well done! And now you wish, perhaps,
To learn of less familiar traps?

Beware of heard, a dreadful word
That looks like beard and sounds like bird,
And dead: it's said like bed, not bead -
For goodness sake don't call it 'deed'!
Watch out for meat and great and threat
(They rhyme with suite and straight and debt.)

Anonymous

THE YOUNG BARD OF JAPAN

There was a young bard of Japan
Whose limericks never would scan;
When they said it was so,

He replied, 'Yes, I know,
But I make a rule of always trying to get just as many words into the last line as I possibly can.'

Anonymous

LEARNING TO READ

I sat there,
And looked glumly at the page,
My mind aching.
I blinked and the tears came.
The book blurred,
Illegible.
The words slowly melted into little rivers
Running past me,
Tauntingly.
The picture smudged,
Like chalk on a blackboard.
The brown vinyl table,
With fake, black, plastic knots,
Gave demure reflections of my crumpled face.
I blinked the tears away.
And concentrated again.
'H ... E ... L ... L ... O,' I sounded.
H..E..L..L..O burned in my mind.
H. E. L. L. O. It stirred long dead fires.
H.E.L.L.O. This word,
This word meant so much.
Then, suddenly, 'Hello!' I cried.
And the world replied ...
'Hello.'

Daniel Ribenfors (Aged 13)

MUSIC

Music is invisible,
invisible as air.
You cannot see it,
cannot touch it,
but you know it's there.

It enters through your ears
and it starts to swirl around.
It seems to fill your body
with its rhythm and its sound.

Music is like magic.
It puts you in a trance.
It sets your body moving
and makes your feelings dance.

Music is a mystery.
It seems to cast a spell.
When music really gets to work
then everything feels well.

Tony Mitton

WORDS I LIKE

Billowing, seaboard, ocean, pearl
Estuary, shale, maroon;
Harlequin, runnel, ripple, swirl,
Labyrinth, lash, lagoon.

Razorbill, cygnet, songbird, kite,
Cormorant, crag, ravine;
Flickering, sun-burst, dappled, flight,
Fiery, dew, serene.

Asteroid, nova, star-dust, moon,
Galaxy, zone, eclipse;
Dynamo, pulsar, planet, rune,
Satellite, spangle, lips.

Boulevard, freeway, turnpike, cruise,
Chevrolet, fin, pavanne;
Tomahawk, firecrest, fantail, fuse,
Saskatchewan, Sioux, Cheyenne.

Tenderness, sweetheart, cherish, miss,
Paramour, fond, befriend;
Family, love, the end.

_____

Steve Turner

HANDS

Hands
handling
dangling in water
making and shaking
slapping and clapping
warming and warning
hitting and fitting
grabbing and rubbing
peeling and feeling
taking and breaking
helping and giving
lifting
sifting sand
hand holding
hand.

Peter Young

HAIR

Hair is brill, hair is brill
Curly hair, Straight hair
Brown hair, Yellow hair
Long hair, Short hair
Parted hair, Messy hair
Hair on chests, hair under arms
Hair on heads, no hair, lots of hair
Hair under noses
Hair today …

                  gone tomorrow.

Aaron Lockwood (Aged 9)

KNEES

I like knees,
bony knees,
wobbly knees,
itchy knees,
neat knees.
I like knees,
bruised knees,
praying knees,
knees with honey on,
knees with jam on,
    knees
      knees
    knees.

Katie Wilson (Aged 6)

JAMAICAN CLAP RHYME

Where your mamma gone?
She gone down town.

She take any money?
She take ten pound.

When your mamma come back,
what she gonna bring back?

Hats and frocks and
shoes and socks.

Anonymous

SOCKS

My local Gents' Outfitter stocks
The latest line in snazzy socks:
Black socks, white socks,
Morning, noon and night socks,
Grey socks, green socks,
Small, large and in between socks,
Blue socks, brown socks,
Always-falling-down socks,
Orange socks, red socks,
Baby socks and bed socks;
Purple socks, pink socks,
What-would-people-think socks,
Holey socks and frayed socks,
British Empire-made socks,
Long socks, short socks,
Any-sort-of-sport socks,
Thick socks, thin socks,
And 'these-have-just-come-in' socks.

Socks with stripes and socks with spots,
Socks with stars and polka dots,
Socks for ankles, socks for knees,
Socks with twelve-month guarantees,
Socks for aunties, socks for uncles,
Socks to cure you of carbuncles,
Socks for nephews, socks for nieces,
Socks that won't show up their creases,
Socks whose colour glows fluorescent,
Socks for child or adolescent,
Socks for ladies, socks for gents,
Socks for only fifty pence.

Socks for winter, socks for autumn,
Socks with garters to support 'em.
Socks for work and socks for leisure,
Socks hand-knitted, made-to-measure,
Socks of wool and polyester,
Socks from Lincoln, Leeds and Leicester,
Socks of cotton and elastic,
Socks of paper, socks of plastic,
Socks of silk-embroidered satin,
Socks with mottoes done in Latin,
Socks for soldiers in the army,
Socks to crochet or macrame,
Socks for destinations distant,
Shrink-proof, stretch-proof, heat-resistant.

Baggy socks, brief socks,
Union Jack motif socks,
Chequered socks, tartan socks,
School or kindergarten socks,
Sensible socks, silly socks,
Frivolous and frilly socks,
Impractical socks, impossible socks,
Drip-dry machine-only-washable socks,
Bulgarian socks, Brazilian socks,
There seem to be over a million socks!

With all these socks, there's just one catch -
It's hard to find a pair that match.

Colin West

ONE OLD OX

One old ox opening oysters,
Two toads totally tired
Trying to trot to Tewkesbury,
Three tame tigers taking tea,
Four fat friars fishing for frogs,
Five fairies finding fire-flies,
Six soldiers shooting snipe,
Seven salmon sailing in Solway,
Eight elegant engineers eating excellent eggs;
Nine nimble noblemen nibbling non-pareils,
Ten tall tinkers tasting tamarinds,
Eleven electors eating early endive,
Twelve tremendous tale-bearers telling truth.

Anonymous

THE SURPRISING NUMBER 37

The number 37 has a special magic to it.
If you multiply 37 x 3, you get   111.
If you multiply 37 x 6, you get   222.
If you multiply 37 x 9, you get   333.
If you multiply 37 x 12, you get   444.
If you multiply 37 x 15, you get   555.
If you multiply 37 x 18, you get   666.
If you multiply 37 x 21, you get   777.
If you multiply 37 x 24, you get   888.
If you multiply 37 x 27, you get   999.

Anonymous

TWO TIMES TABLE

Twice one are two,
Violets white and blue.

Twice two are four,
Sunflowers at the door.

Twice three are six,
Sweet peas on their sticks.

Twice four are eight,
Poppies at the gate.

Twice five are ten,
Pansies bloom again.

Twice six are twelve,
Pinks for those who delve.

Twice seven are fourteen,
Flowers of the runner bean.

Twice eight are sixteen,
Clinging ivy ever green.

Twice nine are eighteen,
Purple thistles to be seen.

Twice ten are twenty,
Hollyhocks in plenty.

Twice eleven are twenty-two,
Daisies wet with morning dew.

Twice twelve are twenty-four,
Roses ... who could ask for more.

Anonymous

THE DREAM OF A BOY WHO LIVED AT NINE ELMS

Nine grenadiers, with bayonets in their guns;
Nine bakers' baskets, with hot-cross buns;
Nine brown elephants, standing in a row;
Nine new velocipedes, good ones to go;
Nine knickerbocker suits, with buttons all complete;
Nine pair of skates with straps for the feet;
Nine clever conjurors eating hot coals;
Nine sturdy mountaineers leaping on their poles;
Nine little drummer-boys beating on their drums;
Nine fat aldermen sitting on their thumbs;
Nine new knockers to our front door;
Nine new neighbours that I never saw before;
Nine times running I dreamt it all plain;
With bread and cheese for supper I could dream it all again!

William Brighty Rands

TWELVE HUNTSMEN

Twelve huntsmen with horns and hounds,
Hunting over other men's grounds!
Eleven ships sailing o'er the main,
Some bound for France and some for Spain;
I wish them all safe home again.
Ten comets in the sky,
Some low and some high;
Nine peacocks in the air,
I wonder how they all came there,
I do not know and I do not care.
Eight joiners in a joiners' hall,
Working with the tools and all;
Seven lobsters in a dish,
As fresh as any heart could wish;
Six beetles against the wall,
Close by an old woman's apple stall;
Five puppies of our dog Ball,
Who daily for their breakfast call;
Four horses stuck in a bog,
Three monkeys tied to a clog;
Two pudding-ends would choke a dog,
With a gaping wide-mouthed waddling frog.

Anonymous

I ASKED THE LITTLE BOY WHO CANNOT SEE

I asked the little boy who cannot see,
'And what is colour like?'
'Why, green,' said he,
'Is like the rustle when the wind blows through
The forest; running water, that is blue;
And red is like a trumpet sound; and pink
Is like the smell of roses; and I think
That purple must be like a thunderstorm;
And yellow is like something soft and warm;
And white is a pleasant stillness when you lie
And dream.'

Anonymous

WHAT IS BLACK?

Black is the night
When there isn't a star
And you can't tell by looking
Where you are.
Black is a pail of paving tar.
Black is jet
And things you'd like to forget.
Black is a chimney
Black is a cat,
A leopard, a raven,
A silk top hat.

The sound of black is
'Boom! Boom! Boom!'
Echoing in
An empty room.
Black is kind -
It covers up
The shabby street,
The broken cup.
Black is the coal
That drives a train
The soot spots on
The window pane.
Black is a feeling
Hard to explain
Like suffering but
Without the pain.
Black is liquorice
And patent leather shoes,
Black is the print
In the news.
Black is beauty
In its deepest form,
The darkest cloud
In a thunderstorm.
Think of what starlight
And lamplight would lack
Diamonds and fireflies
If they couldn't lean against
Black ...

Mary O'Neil

WHAT IS PINK?

What is pink? A rose is pink
By the fountain's brink.
What is red? A poppy's red
In its barley bed.
What is blue? The sky is blue
Where the clouds float through.
What is white? A swan is white
Sailing in the light.
What is yellow? Pears are yellow
Rich and ripe and mellow.
What is green? The grass is green,
With small flowers between.
What is violet? Clouds are violet
In the summer twilight.
What is orange? Why, an orange,
Just an orange!

Christina Rossetti

THE PAINT BOX

'Cobalt and umber and ultramarine,
Ivory black and emerald green -
What shall I paint to give pleasure to you?'
'Paint for me somebody utterly new.'

'I have painted you tigers in crimson and white.'
'The colours were good and you painted aright.'
'I have painted the cook and a camel in blue
And a panther in purple.'   'You painted them true.

Now mix me a colour that nobody knows,
And paint me a country where nobody goes,
And put in it people a little like you,
Watching a unicorn drinking the dew.'

E. V. Rieu

TODAY, IN STRONG COLOURS

Today, in strong colours,
I want you to welcome a visitor.
Give her
A purple wave
A bright red smile
A round of green applause
A royal blue handshake
And a yellow hello.
Place her firmly
On the palette of our friendship.

Sue Cowling

LITTLE BROTHER'S SECRET

When my birthday was coming
Little Brother had a secret
He kept it for days and days
And just hummed a little tune when I asked him.
But one night it rained
And I woke up and heard him crying.
Then he told me
'I planted two lumps of sugar in your garden.
Because you love it so frightfully
I thought there would be a whole sugar tree for your
    birthday
And now it will all be melted.'
O, the darling!

Katherine Mansfield

THE SECRET BROTHER

Jack lived in the green-house
When I was six,
With glass and with tomato plants,
Not with slates and bricks.

I didn't have a brother,
Jack became mine.
Nobody could see him,
He never gave a sign.

Just beyond the rockery,
By the apple-tree,
Jack and his old mother lived,
Only for me.

With a tin telephone
Held beneath the sheet,
I would talk to Jack each night.
We would never meet.

Once my sister caught me,
Said, 'He isn't there.
Down among the flower-pots
Cramm the gardener

Is the only person.'
I said nothing, but
Let her go on talking.
Yet I moved Jack out.

He and his old mother
Did a midnight flit.
No one knew his number:
I had altered it.

Only I could see
The sagging washing-line
And my brother making
Our own secret sign.

Elizabeth Jennings

THE SECRET PLACE

It was my secret place - `
    down at the foot
    of my bed -
    under the covers.

It was very white.

I went there
    with a book, a flashlight,
    and the special pencil
    that my grandfather gave me.

To read -
    and to draw pictures
    on all that white.

It was my secret place
    for about a week -

Until my mother came
    to change the sheets.

Tomie de Paola

JEALOUSY

Jealousy is like a great black
hole sucking everything
in.
Jealousy is like a fungus
growing and growing inside.
Like a monster punching me inside.
Like a star burning up.
Like a bee sting right inside
that's
what
jealousy is

Terry Baylis (Aged 8)

PEARLS

Dad gave me a string of pearls for my birthday.
They aren't real pearls but they look real.
They came nested in deep, deep blue velvet
    in a hinged box with a silvery lid.
His sister had some like them when she was my age.
She was thrilled.
He thought I'd really like them.
I said I did.

I love the box.

Jean Little

TREASURE TROVE

I have a tin
to keep things in
underneath
my bedroom floor.

I put my finger
in the crack,
quietly lift
the floorboard back,

and there's my store,
safely hid
in a tin with roses
on the lid.

A few feathers
and a chicken's claw,
a big tooth
from a dinosaur,

the wrapper
from my Easter egg,
a Christmas robin
with one leg,

long hairs
from a horse's mane,
real pesetas
come from Spain,

three of my
operation stitches,
like spiders
wrapped in bandages,

a marble
full of dragon smoke,
flashing with fire
in the dark,

a magic pebble
round and white,
a sparkler left
from bonfire night.

Underneath
my bedroom floor
there's a treasure tin,
with my things in.

Irene Rawnsley

WALLS I SCREAM

When I went to the Grange for the Ball
And nervously stood in the hall,
I asked of my host,
'Is there maybe a ghost?'
He said 'Nope,' turned, and walked through the wall.

The butler stood straight, pale and tall
And said in half moan and half drawl,
'Hat and coat, if you please,'
Then with consummate ease
He took them away through the wall.

'Well hello there,' I heard a voice call.
For her beauty I'd certainly fall.
Her eyes were beguiling,
Her sweet lips still smiling
As she disappeared through the wall.

My knees knocked. I feared I would fall.
My skin was beginning to crawl,
Couldn't stand any more
So I rushed for the door
That at least would get me through the wall.

'Though her charms would for ever enthrall
I dared not go back there at all.
Then with heart full of terror
I made the grave error
Of driving my car through a wall.

Now I'm also a ghost at the Hall
So why don't you give us a call?
'Though the thought might well daunt you
We'd be delighted to haunt you
And then drive you right up the wall.

Philip C. Gross

VOICE IN THE NIGHT

I listen, listen
as I lie in bed.

Should I pull the covers
over my head?

If I do
then I won't
be able to hear
what it is
that's creeping
near
and nearer
to the house

a ghostly horror
in the night
slithering
slodging
right
beneath my window

but if I don't
hide safe
beneath the sheet
then I'll see it
slothering
over the street
come gaping
in my room
with a ghastly grin

ghoulish-white
gaunt and thin
eyes gleaming red
as bloody pools
glaring inside
black mouth wide
a moor-bleak cave
sharp fangs raised
it's wanting to
hoping to
ready to
taste my blood

I shiver alone
scream silently
wonder why
the vampire
has chosen me

take my fingers
from my ears
as hot tears rise
slide down my cheeks

and hear
a voice outside
crying
out of the darkness
soft
and urgently
'Let me in, our kid!
I've lost my key!'

Joan Poulson

I LIKE

I like to stay up
and listen
when big people talking
jumbie stories

I does feel
so tingly and excited
inside me

But when my mother say
'Girl, time for bed'

Then is when
I does feel a dread

Then is when
I does cover up
from me feet to me head

Then is when
I does wish I didn't listen
to no stupid jumbie story

Then is when
I does wish I did read
me book instead

Grace Nichols

THE WITCH'S CAT

'My magic is dead,' said the witch. 'I'm astounded
That people can fly to the moon and around it.
It used to be mine and the cat's till they found it.
My broomstick is draughty, I snivel with cold
As I ride to the stars. I'm painfully old,
    And so is my cat;
    But planet-and-space-ship,
    Rocket or race-ship
  Never shall part me from that.'

She wrote an advertisement, 'Witch in a fix
Willing to part with the whole bag of tricks,
Going cheap at the price at eighteen and six.'
But no one was ready to empty his coffers
For out-of-date rubbish. There weren't any offers -
    Except for the cat.
    'But planet-and-space-ship,
    Rocket or race-ship
  Never shall part me from that.'

The tears tricked fast, not a sentence she spoke
As she stamped on her broom and the brittle stick broke,
And she dumped in a dustbin her hat and her cloak,
Then clean disappeared, leaving no prints;
And no one at all has set eyes on her since
    Or her tired old cat.
    'But planet-and-space-ship,
    Rocket or race-ship
  Never shall part me from that.'

Ian Serraillier

THE HAIRY TOE

Once there was a woman went out to pick beans,
and she found a Hairy Toe,
She took the Hairy Toe home with her,
and that night, when she went to bed,
the wind began to moan and groan.
Away off in the distance
she seemed to hear a voice crying,
'Who's got my Hair-r-ry To-o-oe?
Who's got my Hair-r-ry To-o-oe?'

The woman scrooched down,
'way down under the covers,
and about that time
the wind appeared to hit the house,
smoosh,
and the old house creaked and cracked
like something was trying to get in.
The voice had come nearer,
almost at the door now,
and it said,
'Where's my Hair-r-ry To-o-oe?
Who's got my Hair-r-ry To-o-oe?'

The woman scrooched further down
under the covers
and pulled them tight around her head.
The wind growled around the house
like some big animal
and r-r-um-mbled
over the chimbley.
All at once she heard the door cr-r-a-ack

and Something slipped in
and began to creep over the floor.
The floor went
cre-e-eak, cre-e-eak
at every step that thing took towards her bed.
The woman could almost feel
it bending over her bed.
Then in an awful voice it said:
'Where's my Hair-r-ry To-o-oe?
Who's got my Hair-r-ry To-o-oe?
You've got it!'

Traditional

THE WITCH AND THE AA MAN

Old Peggotty Witch had a problem -
she had to reach Blackpond by eight.
The Witches' Convention would start then,
and nobody liked to be late.

Her broomstick refused to get going,
although it had made many flights.
She kicked at the twigs in frustration,
but that only laddered her tights.

The usual words to get airborne
she'd said twenty times,
maybe more.
But never a twitch did the broom make.
It stayed, looking dead, on the floor.

But then she remembered the AA,
and gave them a telephone call.
And soon a young fellow was standing,
with toolbox,
in Peggotty's hall.

He hadn't much knowledge of broomsticks,
so didn't know what to check first.
They don't have an engine or cables,
or things that can fracture or burst.

It didn't require any petrol.
No handbrake was holding it back.
And nothing new could be discovered
by raising it up on a jack.

But this was a thoughtful young fellow -
most helpful and enthusiastic.
A catapult start he suggested,
but that needed too much elastic.

Now Peggotty Witch had the sniffles -
a cold she had suffered all week -
and anyone's nose,
when it's blocked up,
affects how they sound when they speak.

'That's it!' said the AA man brightly.
'Your words
must have sounded most weird.
Have a mint,'
and he gave her a strong one,
so her poor bunged-up nose
quickly cleared.

Then: 'LICKERTY-SPLIT!'
she was airborne,
shooting of with a wave and a grin.
She went supersonic to Blackpond,
coming down with a loop and a spin.

Meanwhile,
back at AA headquarters,
the young man was giving some hints.
'You don't need a toolbox
for broomsticks,' he said.
'Just a packet of very strong mints.'

Barry Buckingham

QUEEN NEFERTITI

Spin a coin, spin a coin,
    All fall down;
Queen Nefertiti
    Stalks through the town.

Over the pavements
    Her feet go clack,
Her legs are as tall
    As a chimney stack;

Her fingers flicker
    Like snakes in the air,
The walls split open
    At her green-eyed stare;

Her voice is thin
    As the ghosts of bees;
She will crumble your bones,
    She will make your blood freeze.

Spin a coin, spin a coin,
    All fall down;
Queen Nefertiti
    Stalks through the town.

Anonymous

THE SPELLER'S BAG

Here a bone.
Here a stone.
In my bag
I keep them all.

A stone brought me
by the sea.
A bone taken from where
I'll never tell thee.

A bone, a stone,
a feather, a shell,
all in my bag
to cast a spell.

A shell that taught
the wind to howl.
A feather stolen
from the back of an owl.

Then again it might be
from a raven's neck.
I'll never tell thee.

Look inside all who dare.

Inside my bag
you'll find your fear.

John Agard

THE SLEEPY GIANT

My age is three hundred and seventy-two,
    And I think, with the deepest regret,
How I used to pick up and voraciously chew
    The dear little boys whom I met.

I've eaten them raw, in their holiday suits;
    I've eaten them curried with rice;
I've eaten them baked, in their jackets and boots,
    And found them exceedingly nice.

But now that my jaws are too weak for such fare,
    I think it exceedingly rude
To do such a thing, when I'm quite well aware
    Little boys do not like to be chewed.

And so I contentedly live upon eels,
    And try to do nothing amiss,
And I pass all the time I can spare from my meals
    In innocent slumber - like this.

Charles E. Carryl

A SPELL FOR SLEEPING

Sweet william, silverweed, sally-my-handsome.
Dimity darkens the pittering water.
On gloomed lawns wanders a king's daughter.

Curtains are clouding the casement windows.
A moon-glade smurrs the lake with light.
Doves cover the tower with quiet.

Three owls whit-whit in the withies.
Seven fish in a deep pool shimmer.
The princess moves to the spiral stair.

Slowly the sickle moon mounts up.
Frogs hump under moss and mushroom.
The princess climbs to her high hushed room,

Step by step to her shadowed tower.
Water laps the white lake shore.
A ghost opens the princess's door.

    Seven fish in the sway of the water.
    Six candles for a king's daughter.
    Five sighs for a drooping head.
    Four ghosts to gentle her bed.
    Three owls in the dusk falling.
    Two tales to be telling.
    One spell for sleeping.

Tamarisk, trefoil, tormentil.
Sleep rolls down from the clouded hill.
A princess dreams of a silver pool.

The moonlight spreads, the soft ferns flitter.
Stilled in a shimmering drift of water,
Seven fish dream of a lost king's daughter.

Alastair Reid

WHOPPERS

'I'm having a pony for Christmas,
And a meal at a posh hotel.'
'That's nothing, I'm having a video,
and two colour tellies as well.'

'My dad's having a Rolls Royce car.'
'Well, my dad's having two -
One for his window-cleaning gear
And one for mum - brand new.'

'My mum's having a baby.'
'Well, my mum's having twins -
Or maybe she'll have triplets,
Or even quads or quins.'

'I'm having a sailing dinghy:
Cor, won't the neighbours go green!'
'We're having the yacht Britannia
Bought secondhand from the Queen.'

'We're off to the Costa Brava,
Dad's getting tickets quite soon.'
'I'll think of you then while we're on
Our luxury tour of the moon.'

.....

'To tell you the truth, I've been fibbing
And boasting, I realize.'
'That's nothing: I've not been telling fibs,
But monstrous, walloping lies!'

Eric Finney

UNEMPLOYABLE

'I usth thu work in the thircusth,'
He said,
Between the intermittent showers that
emerged from his mouth.
'Oh,' I said, 'what did you do?'
'I usth thu catcth bulleth in my theeth.'

Gareth Owen

IT'S RAINING CATS AND DOGS

It's raining cats and dogs -
The sky is growing dark,
Instead of pitter-patter
It's splatter, yowl and bark.

Bulldogs bounce on bonnets,
Alsatians hang in trees,
Poodles land on policemen
And bring them to their knees.

Tabby cats come squealing
Like rockets overhead,
Siamese look worried
At pavements turning red.

It's raining cats and dogs,
Although it shouldn't oughta.
Next time I pray for rain,
I'll add that I mean water.

Steve Turner

I'VE NEVER HEARD
THE QUEEN SNEEZE

I've never heard the Queen sneeze
Or seen her blow her nose,
I've never seen her pick a spot
Or tread on someone's toes,
I've never seen her slide upon
A slippery piece of ice,
I've never seen her frown and say
'This jelly is not nice!'
I've never seen her stick a finger
In her royal and waxy ear,
I've never seen her take it out
And sniff, and say 'Oh dear!'
I've never seen her swop her jewels
Or play frisbee with her crown,
I've never seen her spill her soup
Or drop porridge on her gown.
I wonder what she does
When she sits at home alone,
Playing with her corgis
And throwing them a bone?
I bet they've seen the Queen sneeze
And seen her blow her nose,
I bet they've seen her pick a spot
And tread on someone's toes.
I bet they've seen her slide upon
A slippery piece of ice,
I bet they've seen her fown and say,
'This jelly is not nice!'
I bet they've seen her stick a finger

In her royal and waxy ear,
I bet they've seen her take it out
And sniff, and say 'Oh dear!'
I bet they've seen her swop her jewels
And play frisbee with her crown,
I bet they've seen her spill her soup
And drop porridge on her gown.
So why can't I do all these things
Without being sent to bed?
Or failing that, why can't I
Be made the Queen instead?

Brian Patten

WANTED

WANTED: PAPER
BOYS AND GIRLS

So the notice said.

And who can blame them?
Think of the benefits
over slugs and snails,
or even,
sugar and spice.

Michael Harrison

ST. GEORGE AND THE DRAGON

St. George looked at the dragon
And much to his surprise,
He noticed that the dragon
Had large appealing eyes.
'Pardon me,' said brave St. George,
'I hear you're cruel and sly.'
'Oh no, not me,' the dragon said,
'I wouldn't hurt a fly.'
'I've come to slay you,' said St. George,
'And save the maiden fair
That you have captured, and no doubt
Imprisoned in your lair.'
'I used to be both cruel and sly,
Of that there is no doubt,'
Replied the dragon, 'but not now,
My fire has all burnt out.
The maiden you have come to save
Has made a pet of me.
She takes me walkies on a lead
And feeds me cups of tea.
So if you want to do brave deeds
The like of which I've read,
Please take the maiden home with you,
And so save me instead.'

Finola Akister

FISHERMAN'S TALE

By the canal
I was quietly fishing
when a bowler hat
floated by,
stopped level with my eye
and began to rise.

Below it was a man's head
wearing spectacles;
he asked
'This way to Brackley?'
'Straight ahead.'
The face sank back
beneath the wet,
but I was thinking
Brackley's seven miles,
it's getting late;
perhaps he doesn't know
how far.

I tapped the hat
with my rod; again
the face rose; 'Yes?'
'You'll need to hurry
to arrive before dark.'
'Don't worry,' he said;
I'm on my bike.'

Irene Rawnsley

IMAGINE

If the sea was in the sky,
And trees grew underground,
And if all fish had giant teeth,
And all the cows were round;
If birds flew backwards all the time,
And vultures ruled the land.
If bricks poured down instead of rain,
If all there was was sand;
If every man had seven heads
And we spoke Double Dutch,
And if the sun came out at night,
I wouldn't like it much.

Anonymous

QUEER THINGS

'Very, very queer things have been happening to me
 In some of the places where I've been.
I went to the pillar-box this morning with a letter
 And a hand came out and took it in.

'When I got home again I thought I'd have
 A glass of spirits to steady myself;
And I take my bible oath, but that bottle and glass
 Came a-hopping down off the shelf.

'No, no, I says, I'd better take no spirits,
 And I sat down to have a cup of tea;
And blowed if my old pair of carpet-slippers
 Didn't walk across the carpet to me!

'So I took my newspaper and went into the park,
 And looked round to see no one was near,
When a voice right out of the middle of the paper
 Started reading the news bold and clear!

'Well, I guess there's some magician out to help me,
 So perhaps there's no need for alarm;
And if I manage not to anger him,
 Why should he do me any harm?'

James Reeves

THE SPANGLED PANDEMONIUM

The spangled pandemonium
Is missing from the zoo.
He bent the bars the barest bit,
And slithered glibly through.

He crawled across the moated wall,
He climbed the mango tree,
And when the keeper scrambled up,
He nipped him in the knee.

To all of you, a warning
Not to wander after dark,
Or if you must, make very sure
You stay out of the park.

For the spangled pandemonium
Is missing from the zoo,
And since he nipped his keeper,
He would just as soon nip you.

Palmer Brown

A TRAGIC STORY

There lived a sage in days of yore,
And he a handsome pigtail wore:
But wondered much, and sorrowed more,
    Because it hung behind him.

He mused upon this curious case,
And swore he'd change the pigtail's place,
And have it hanging at his face,
    Not dangling there behind him.

Says he, 'The mystery I've found -
I'll turn me round,' - he turned him round;
    But still it hung behind him.

Then round, and round, and out and in,
All day the puzzled sage did spin;
In vain - it mattered not a pin -
    The pigtail hung behind him.

And right and left, and round about,
And up and down, and in and out,
He turned; but still the pigtail stout
    Hung steadily behind him.

And though his efforts never slack,
And though he twist, and twirl, and tack,
Alas! still faithful to his back,
    The pigtail hangs behind him.

William Makepeace Thackeray

THE RELENTLESS PURSUIT OF THE 12-TOED SNORTIBLOG!

It SNIFFS you out: 'sffft, sffft, sffft'
It HEARS your heartbeat: 'dup dup dup'
It SEES your terror: 'aaaaaah!'
It TASTES revenge: 'mmmmmmmmmmm'

It will give you a big kiss:
　　'SHSPPLUKKLSSMLOOPSCHPPWASSSSHLAKKK'!

Anonymous

WHEN FISHES SET UMBRELLAS UP

When fishes set umbrellas up
　　If the rain-drops run,
Lizards will want their parasols
　　To shade them from the sun.

The peacock has a score of eyes,
　　With which he cannot see;
The cod-fish has a silent sound,
　　However that may be.

No dandelions tell the time
　　Although they turn to clocks;
Cat's cradle does not hold the cat,
　　Nor foxglove fit the fox.

Christina Rossetti

THE QUANGLE WANGLE'S HAT

On the top of the Crumpetty Tree
    The Quangle Wangle sat,
But his face you could not see,
    On account of his Beaver Hat.
For his Hat was a hundred and two feet wide,
    With ribbons and bibbons on every side
And bells, and buttons, and loops, and lace,
    So that nobody ever could see the face
    Of the Quangle Wangle Quee.

The Quangle Wangle said
    To himself on the Crumpetty tree, -
'Jam and jelly and bread
    Are the best food for me!
But the longer I live on this Crumpetty Tree
The plainer than ever it seems to me
That very few people come this way
And that life on the whole is far from gay!'
    Said the Quangle Wangle Quee.

But there came to the Crumpetty Tree,
    Mr and Mrs Canary;
And they said - 'Did you ever see
    Any spot so charmingly airy?
May we build a nest on your lovely Hat?
Mr Quangle Wangle, grant us that!
O please let us come and build a nest
Of whatever material suits you best,
    Mr Quangle Wangle Quee!'

And besides, to the Crumpetty Tree
    Came the Stork, the Duck, and the Owl;
The Snail, and the Bumble-Bee,
    The Frog, and the Fimble Fowl;
(The Fimble Fowl, with a Corkscrew leg;)
And all of them said, - 'We humbly beg,
    We may build our homes on your lovely Hat, -
Mr. Quangle Wangle, grant us that!
    Mr Quangle Wangle Quee!'

And the Golden Grouse came there,
    And the Pobble who has no toes, -
And the small Olympian bear, -
    And the Dong with a luminous nose.
And the Blue Baboon, who played the flute, -
And the Orient Calf from the land of Tute, -
And the Attery Squash, and the Bisky Bat, -
All came and built on the lovely hat
    Of the Quangle Wangle Quee.

And the Quangle Wangle said
    To himself on the Crumpetty Tree, -
'When all these creatures move
    What a wonderful noise there'll be!'
And at night by the light of the Mulberry moon
They danced to the Flute of the Blue Baboon,
On the broad green leaves of the Crumpetty Tree,
And all were as happy as happy could be,
    With the Quangle Wangle Quee.

Edward Lear

GUARDIAN

Sprawled across the stair
the cat blocks my way.

Shoo! I nearly say
but the sun in which

he basks gilds the rich
colours of the stained

glass window behind
him and the brief gleam

has briefly turned him
into a tiger.

Keith Bosley

SLEEPING CATS

Cats dedicate
their lives
to dozing,

stretched out like
pulled gum before
the gas fire,

parcelled up,
legs folded away
like stored tent poles,

tail tucked under,
slitted eyes watching
what will happen next,

curled into doughnuts
on doorsteps,
on walls and window ledges,

drowsing,
too hot to purr,
in smelted sunlight,

snoozing, half-awake,
murpling in ecstasy
on lazy laps,

or lying heavy
as bags of cement
on warm beds

in the murk of night,
deeply asleep,
for once.

Like Eskimos
with all their words
for whiteness,

cats have dozens
of different ways
of sleeping.

Moira Andrew

THE CATS OF KILKENNY

There were once two cats of Kilkenny,
Each thought there was one cat too many;
So they fought and they fit,
And they scratched and they bit,
Till, excepting their nails
And the tips of their tails,
Instead of two cats, there weren't any.

Anonymous

MY CAT

My cat
got fatter
and fatter.
I didn't know
what was the matter.
Then,
know what she did?
She went into the cupboard
and hid.

She was fat when she went in,
but she came out
thin.
I had a peep.
Know what I saw?
Little kittens
all in a heap

- 1 - 2 - 3 - 4

My cat's great.

Nigel Gray

BUMBLEFOOT

Our dog Bumblefoot
is huge and hopeless.
When he stands on his hind legs
he is two metres tall,
but he is clumsier than a clown
and excessively stupid. He doesn't know
the meaning of 'stay' or 'heel.'

Inside the house
he is a bull in a china shop.
His massive tail
upends the ornaments on shelves and tables
and sweeps them to destruction.
He leaves a muddy trail across the floor
like the fossil footprints of a dinosaur,
but he is always happy,
grinning lopsidedly in rare good humour.
He terrorises the district
with friendliness.

When visitors arrive
he greets them roisterously,
puts his paws on their shoulders
and starts to kiss their cheeks.
If they fall over backwards
he stands on them and licks them ecstatically
from chin to forehead with his wide tongue
like a wet squeegee.

When Uncle Mike at last regains his feet -
so furious that he'd really like to brain him -
he mops himself and asks sarcastically,
'How long did it take to train him ?'

Colin Thiele

ROGER THE DOG

Asleep he wheezes at his ease.
He only wakes to scratch his fleas.

He hogs the fire, he bakes his head
As if it were a loaf of bread.

He's just a sack of snoring dog.
You can lug him like a log.

You can roll him with your foot,
He'll stay snoring where he's put.

I take him out for exercise,
He rolls in cowclap up to his eyes.

He will not race, he will not romp,
He saves his strength for gobble and chomp.

He'll work as hard as you could wish
Emptying his dinner dish,

Then flops flat, and digs down deep,
Like a miner, into sleep.

———————
Ted Hughes

BURYING THE DOG IN THE GARDEN

When we buried
the dog in
the garden on
the grave we put
a cross and
the tall man
next door was
cross.
'Animals have no
souls,' he said.
'They must have animal
souls,' we said. 'No,'
he said and
shook his head.
'Do you need a
soul to go
to Heaven?' we
asked. He nodded
his head. 'Yes,'
he said.
'That means my
hamster's not
in Heaven,' said
Kevin. 'Nor is
my dog,' I said.
'My cat could sneak
in anywhere,' said
Clare. And we thought
what a strange place Heaven
must be with
nothing to stroke

for eternity.
We were all
seven.
We decided we
did not want to
go to Heaven.
For that the
tall man next
door is to blame.

Brian Patten

MARE

When the mare shows you
her yellow teeth, stuck
with clover and gnawed leaf,
you know they have combed
pastures of spiky grasses,
and tough thickets.

But when you offer her
a sweet, white lump
from the trembling plate
of your palm - she trots
to the gate, sniffs -
and takes it with velvet lips.

Judith Thurman

THE FROG

What a wonderful bird the frog are -
When he sit, he stand almost;
When he hop, he fly almost.
He ain't got no sense hardly;
He ain't got no tail hardly either.
When he sit, he sit on what he ain't
got - almost.

Anonymous

BLUE TITS

have lemony waistcoats, clown-white, round-bearded faces,
skullcaps and eyes that glint like ball bearings

somersault, trapeze, trampoline - twig to leaf, leaf to twig,
(evanescent, light as raindrops)

clamp under coconut caves, straddle cake smithereens,
their tiny rakish claws steel-delicate -

throw eyes over shoulders, flick back in time
to snap scissor-beaked at scrounging relatives

but themselves only snatch between eyeshots -
not to be part of tomorrow's feline gut.

Geoffrey Holloway

THE HEN

The Hen is a ferocious fowl,
She pecks you till she makes you howl.

And all the time she flaps her wings,
And says the most insulting things.

And when you try to take her eggs,
She bites large pieces from your legs.

The only safe way to get these,
Is to creep on your hands and knees.

In the meanwhile a friend must hide,
And jump out on the other side.

And then you snatch the eggs and run,
While she pursues the other one.

The difficulty is, to find
A trusty friend who will not mind.

Lord Alfred Douglas

THE HERON

I said to the heron, 'Why do you stand
In that swift-flowing stream in the pebbles and sand
On only one foot?
I'd have thought it would be more convenient to put
Both feet in the stream while you patiently seek
The silvery fish to spear with your beak?'

The heron glared back and his voice quickly rose,
'I'd have thought it was something that everyone knows:
In a warm, feathered hollow one foot I now hold
Because swift-flowing streams are excessively cold.'

Gregory Harrison

LIFE AS
A SHEEP

Sometimes
Oi stands
Sometimes
Oi sits
Then
Stands again
Then
Sits
For a bit.

Sometimes
Oi wanders
Sometimes
Oi stays
Sometimes
Oi chews
Sometimes
Oi strays.

Sometimes
Oi coughs
Sometimes
Oi don't
Sometimes
Oi bleats

Sometimes
Oi won't.
Sometimes
Oi watch
The human race
Or
Smiles to meself
Or
Stares into space

And when
Oi's happy
Oi'd dance and sing
But Oi
Don't have the knack
To do
Such a thing.

At night
Oi lays
By the old church
steeple
And
Falls asleep
By counting people.

Gareth Owen

ANNE AND THE FIELD-MOUSE

We found a mouse in the chalk quarry today
In a circle of stones and empty oil drums
By the fag ends of a fire. There had been
A picnic there; he must have been after the crumbs.

Jane saw him first, a flicker of brown fur
In and out of the charred wood and chalk-white.
I saw him last, but not till we'd turned up
Every stone and surprised him into flight.

Though not far - little zigzag spurts from stone
To stone. Once, as he lurked in his hiding-place,
I saw his beady eyes uplifted to mine.
I'd never seen such terror in so small a face.

I watched, amazed and guilty. Beside us suddenly
A heavy pheasant whirred up from the ground,
Scaring us all; and, before we knew it, the mouse
Had broken cover, skimming away without a sound,

Melting into the nettles. We didn't go
Till I'd chalked in capitals on a rusty can:
THERE'S A MOUSE IN THOSE NETTLES LEAVE
HIM ALONE. NOVEMBER 15th. ANNE

Ian Serraillier

FIRST FOX

A big fox stands in the spring grass,
Glossy in the sun, chestnut bright,
Plumb centre of the open meadow, a leaf
From a picturebook.

Forepaws delicately nervous,
Thick brush on the grass
He rakes the air for the scent
Of the train rushing by.

My first fox,
Wiped from my eye,
In a moment of train-
time.

Pamela Gillilan

FABLE

The mountain and the squirrel
had a quarrel;
and the former called the latter 'Little Prig.'
Bun replied,
'You are doubtless very big;
But all sorts of things and weather
Must be taken in together,
To make up a year
And a sphere.
And I think it no disgrace
To occupy my place.
If I'm not so large as you,
You are not so small as I,
And not half so spry.
I'll not deny you make
A very pretty squirrel track;
Talents differ; all is well and wisely put;
If I cannot carry forests on my back,
Neither can you crack a nut.'

Ralph Waldo Emerson

THE BAT

By day the bat is cousin to the mouse.
He likes the attic of an aging house.

His fingers make a hat about his head.
His pulse beat is so slow we think him dead.

He loops in crazy figures half the night
Among the trees that face the corner light.

But when he brushes up against a screen,
We are afraid of what our eyes have seen;

For something is amiss or out of place
When mice with wings can wear a human face.

Theodore Roethke

CAMEL

O camel in the zoo.
You don't do any of the things
They tell me that you used to do
In Egypt, and in other lands,
Carrying potentates and kings
Across the burning desert sand
With gorgeous trappings made of blue
And scarlet silks to cover you.

Your humps are carried on your back
Just the way they always were,
You thrust your old head up and back,
And make your neck go in and out,
And spill the foam upon your fur,
And writhe and jerk and rear about,
But kneel no more upon the sands
To mount the kings of Eastern lands.

May Britton Miller

THE PYRAMIDS

                              I
                            know
                         that the
                    usual explanation
               for the existence of pyramids
            in Egypt is that they were monuments
         to some Pharaoh or other, but the truth is this:
      camels are known as the ships of the desert, right?
   Well, obviously the pyramids were really lighthouses
to stop camels from crashing into the Sphinx, and stuff like that.

Mike Jubb

IF YOU SHOULD MEET A CROCODILE

If you should meet a Crocodile
Don't take a stick and poke him;
Ignore the welcome in his smile,
Be careful not to stroke him.
For as he sleeps upon the Nile,
He thinner gets and thinner;
And whene'er you meet a Crocodile
He's ready for his dinner.

Anonymous

GERALDINE GIRAFFE

The
longest
ever
woolly
scarf
was
worn
by Geraldine
Giraffe.
Around
her
neck
the
scarf
she wound,
but
still
it
trailed
upon
the
ground.

Colin West

THE PARROT

The deep affections of the breast
    That Heaven to living things imparts
Are not exclusively possessed
    By human hearts.

A parrot from the Spanish Main,
    Full young and early caged, came o'er
With bright wings to the black domain
    Of Mulla's shore.

To spicy groves where he had won
    His plumage of resplendent hue,
His native fruits and skies and sun,
    He bade adieu.

For these he changed the smoke of turf,
    A heathery land and misty sky,
And turned on rocks and raging surf
    His golden eye.

But petted, in our climate cold
    He lived and chattered many a day;
Until with age from green and gold
    His wings grew grey.

At last, when blind and seeming dumb,
    He scolded, laughed, and spoke no more,
A Spanish stranger chanced come
    To Mulla's shore.

He hailed the bird in Spanish speech;
    The bird in Spanish speech replied,
Flapped round his cage with joyous screech,
    Dropped down, and died.

Thomas Campbell

TWO OCTOPUSES GOT MARRIED

Two octopuses got married and walked down the aisle
Arm in arm in arm in arm in arm in arm in arm in arm
in arm in arm in arm in arm in arm in arm in arm in arm

Remy Charlip

WHO WILL GO FIRST?

We'll go first, said the ants
Because we are the smallest.

No, I'll go first, said Elephant
Because I'm the heaviest.

Sorry, but I'll go first, said the
Monkey.

No, said Noah
Giraffe is first, because his neck
has been hurting.

Kevin Horton (Aged 7)

CHAMELEONS

Chameleons are seldom seen,
They're red, they're orange, then they're green.
They're one of nature's strangest sights,
Their colours change like traffic lights.

Colin West

SPRING FJORD

I was out in my kayak
I was out at sea in it
I was paddling
very gently in the fjord Ammasssivik
there was ice in the water
and on the water a petrel
turned his head this way that way
didn't see me paddling
Suddenly nothing but his tail
then nothing
He plunged but not for me:
huge head upon the water
great hairy seal
giant head with giant eyes, moustache
all shining and dripping
and the seal came gently toward me
Why didn't I harpoon him?
Was I sorry for him?
was it the day, the spring day, the seal
playing in the sun
like me?

_____

Traditional Inuit Song

THE LIGHTHOUSE

What I remember best about
my holiday was how, each night,
the lighthouse kept sweeping my bedroom
with its clean, cool ray of light.

I lay there, tucked up in the blankets,
and suddenly the lighthouse shone:
a switched on torch that stabbed the night
like a murderer and moved on.

Then back it came, out of the dark,
and swung round, as in some fixed plan:
the light of the lighthouse - opening,
folding, and closing like a fan.

Raymond Wilson

CORAL

'O sailor, come ashore,
    What have you brought for me?'
'Red coral, white coral,
    Coral from the sea.'

'I did not dig it from the ground,
    Nor pluck it from the tree;
Feeble insects made it
    In the stormy sea.'

Christina Rossetti

THAT SINKING FEELING

He rocked the boat,
Did Ezra Shank;
These bubbles mark
O
O
O
O
O
O
O
O
O
O
O
O
O
O
O
O
O
O
O
O
O
Where Ezra sank.

Anonymous

THE MONSTER

I saw the great sea
       gnawing -
          gnawing at pebbles -
chewing the sand
   and spitting
      the wet sea-wrack.

I saw the great sea
       making
          his rolling patterns,
coming and going,
   rising
      and falling back.

I heard the great sea
      hissing as geese do;
          running
over my toes
   and ankles,
      cold as a knife,

I felt his sharp tongue
      creeping and crawling
          upwards -
knee high
   waist high ... then
      I ran for my life!

Jean Kenward

SEA TIMELESS SONG

Hurricane come
and hurricane go
but sea - sea timeless
sea timeless
sea timeless
sea timeless
sea timeless

Hibiscus bloom
then dry-wither so
but sea - sea timeless
sea timeless
sea timeless
sea timeless
sea timeless

Tourist come
and tourist go
but sea - sea timeless
sea timeless
sea timeless
sea timeless
sea timeless

Grace Nichols

HOW TO MAKE A SAILOR'S PIE

'Tell me, pray, if you may how to make a sailor's pie?'
'First, then, you must take a teacup full of sky!
A strand of hemp, a silent star
And the wind's lullaby,
A flake of foam, a scent of night
And a gull's cry;
A taste of salt, a touch of tar
And a sorrowful goodbye:
Mix all these together, to make a sailor's pie.'

Joan Aiken

OLD MAN OCEAN

Old Man Ocean, how do you pound
Smooth glass rough, rough stones round?
Time and the tide and the wild waves rolling.
Night and the wind and the long grey dawn.

Old Man Ocean, what do you tell,
What do you sing in the empty shell?
Fog and the storm and the long bell tolling,
Bones in the deep and the brave men gone

Russell Hoban

THE WALK

Yesterday
Our class visited the sea-shore
To search for sea creatures
And a whole lot more
But all we found were

Plastic toys, teddies and cubes
Tin cans, squashed and empty
Crisp paper bags and bottle tops
Polystyrene that will never rot
All this in one afternoon
On the sea-shore
A whole lot of pollution
And not much more

Michelle Walker (Aged 7)

GOLIATH

They chop down 100 ft trees
To make chairs
I bought one
I am six foot one inch.
When I sit in the chair
I'm four foot two.
Did they really chop down a 100 ft tree
To make me look shorter?

Spike Milligan

'MUMMY, OH MUMMY'

'Mummy, Oh Mummy, what's this pollution
That everyone's talking about?'
'Pollution's the mess that the country is in,
That we'd all be far better without.
It's factories belching their fumes in the air,
And the beaches all covered with tar,
Now throw all those sweet papers into the bushes
Before we get back in the car.'

'Mummy, Oh Mummy, who makes pollution,
And why don't they stop if it's bad?'
''Cos people like that just don't think about others,
They don't think at all, I might add.
They spray all the crops and they poison the flowers,
And wipe out the birds and the bees,
Now there's a good place we could dump that old mattress
Right out of sight in the trees.'

'Mummy, Oh Mummy, what's going to happen
If all the pollution goes on?'
'Well the world will end up like a second-hand junk-yard,
With all of its treasures quite gone.
The fields will be littered with plastics and tins,
The streams will be covered with foam,
Now throw those two pop bottles over the hedge,
Save us from carting them home.'

'But Mummy, Oh Mummy, if I throw the bottles,
Won't that be polluting the wood?'
'Nonsense! that isn't the same thing at all,
You just shut up and be good.

If you're going to start getting silly ideas
I'm taking you home right away,
'Cos pollution is something that other folk do,
We're just enjoying our day.'

Anonymous

TIGER IN A ZOO

She stalks a steel-branched jungle
And paces concrete grass,
Though her stripes afford poor camouflage
Behind the metal bars.

She paces concrete grass
And sees the horizon shimmer
As beyond the city's drizzle,
The distant mountains glimmer.

She sees the horizon shimmer
Beneath the uncaged sky
And hunts a shadow antelope
As spectral vultures fly.

Beneath an uncaged sky
My imagination stirs,
But the zoo is her world
And has always been;
And the dreams are mine
Not hers.

Pat Moon

AN ALPHABET FOR THE PLANET

A for air.
The gentle breeze by which we live.
B for bread.
A food to bake, and take -- and *give*.
C for climate.
It can be warm, it can be cold, ...
D for dolphin.
A smiling friend no net should hold.
E for Earth.
Our ship through space, and home to share.
F for family,
Which also means people *everywhere*.
G for green.
Colour of life we'll help to spread.
H for healthy.
Happy and strong, no fumes with lead.
I for ivory.
The elephant's tusks, his *own* to keep.
J for jungle.
A rainforest. No axe should creep.
K for kindly.
To everyone, gentle and good.
L for life.
It fills the sea and town and wood.
M for mother.
She may feel hurt, but loves us all.
N for nest.
A tiny home for chicks so small.
O for Ozone.
It shields our Earth from harmful rays.
P for peace.
'My happy dream,' the Planet says.

Q for quiet.
Where no loud noise can get at you.
R for recycled.
Old cans and cards as good as new.
S for Sun.
The nearest star. It gives us light.
T for tree.
A grander plant, a green delight.
U for united.
Working as one to put things right.
V for victory.
 Winning over disease and war.
    W for water.
       The whole earth drinks when rainclouds pour.
        X for Xylophone.
           Music from wood -- the high notes soar!
           Y for yummy.
             Those tasty fruits 'organically grown.'
             Z for zoo.
             A cage, a condor -- sad, alone.

Riad Nourallah

HOW CAN ONE SELL THE AIR?

We shall consider your offer
to buy our land.
What is it that the White Man wants to buy?
My people will ask.

How can one sell the air
or buy the warmth of the earth?
It is difficult for us to imagine.
If we don't own the sweet air
or the bubbling water,
how can you buy it from us?
Each hillside of pines shining in the sun,
each sandy beach and rocky river bank,
every steep valley with bees humming
or mists hanging in dark woods,
has been made sacred by some event
in the memory of our people.

We are part of the earth
and the earth is part of us.
The fragrant flowers are our sisters;
the reindeer, the horse,
the great eagles, are our brothers.
The foamy crests of waves in the river,
the sap of meadow flowers,
the pony's sweat and the man's sweat
are one and the same thing.
So when the Great Chief in Washington
sends word that he wants to buy all these things,
we find it hard to understand.

Chief Seattle

REAL LIFE

'Yes,' thought John
his eyes gleaming with excitement
as he looked round the ancient Inn
on the edge of the moors
that was connected to
otherwise inaccessible St Peter's Cove
which had once been a haunt of smugglers
by a secret underground passage
from his bedroom
and which his strange Aunty Lucy
had rented to his mother and father
and Uncle David for
the whole summer holidays,
'Yes this looks just the sort
of place for an adventure but
that kind of thing
only happens in books.'
And he was right.

Gareth Owen

GOODBYE GRANNY

Goodbye Granny
it's nearly time to fly
goodbye Granny
I am going in the sky.
I have my suitcase
and things.
You have packed
me everything
except the sunshine.
All our good times
are stored
up inside
more than enough
for any plane ride.
Goodbye Granny
things will be all right
goodbye Granny
I won't forget to write.
Goodbye Granny
bye! bye!
bye! bye!

Pauline Stewart

A TRIP TO MORROW

I started on a journey just about a week ago
For the little town of Morrow in the State of Ohio.
I never was a traveller and really didn't know
That Morrow had been ridiculed a century or so.
I went down to the depot for my ticket and applied
For tips regarding Morrow, interviewed the station guide.
Said I, 'My friend, I want to go to Morrow and return
Not later than to-morrow, for I haven't time to burn.'

Said he to me, 'Now let me see, if I have heard you right,
You want to go to Morrow and come back to-morrow night,
You should have gone to Morrow yesterday and back to-day,
For if you started yesterday to Morrow, don't you see
You should have got to Morrow and returned to-day at three.
The train that started yesterday, now understand me right,
To-day it gets to Morrow and returns to-morrow night.'

'Now if you start to Morrow, you will surely land
To-morrow into Morrow, not to-day you understand,
For the train to-day to Morrow, if the schedule is right
Will get you into Morrow by about to-morrow night.'
Said I, 'I guess you know it all, but kindly let me say,
How can I go to Morrow if I leave the town to-day?'
Said he, 'You cannot go to Morrow any more to-day,
For the train that goes to Morrow is a mile upon its way.'

Anonymous

OVERTAKING

acar   avan acaravan
    acar avan acaravan
    avan acar acaravan
    avan acar acaravan
    avan acar acaravan
    avan acaravan acar
      avan acaravan   acar

Ian Larmont

'ARE WE NEARLY THERE YET?'

We got on the coach for London,
Hoping we'd see the tower,
We sat on the coach for ages,
We sat on the coach for hours.

We eventually got to cold Trafalgar Square,
Our hands were all a quiver,
We ate our lunch on the banks of the Thames,
But Tom's floated off down the river.

We were all very sensible,
But Jake was a bit of a danger,

It was great strolling up Downing Street,
And having tea and buns with John Major.

We walked past 'Planet Hollywood',
And saw a rather suspicious barman,
We had great fun in the British Museum,
And a long chat with Tutankhamun.

We saw Nelson on his column,
The highlight of the day,
And looking at Buckingham Palace,
I think we got a wave.

We got back on the coach for home,
Saying 'Cheerio' to Big Ben,
But the phrase that was asked throughout the coach was,
'Are we nearly there yet?' again ... and again and ... again.

Lucie Davis (Aged 11)

IF ONLY I COULD DRIVE A TRAIN

If only I could drive a train
I'd fit it with computers
And take off on a mystery tour
To startle bored commuters,
And how they'd gaze and mutter
As we flew between the stars
To pull in, only two hours late,
At platform four on Mars.

Richard Edwards

FROM A RAILWAY CARRIAGE

Faster than fairies, faster than witches,
Bridges and houses, hedges and ditches;
And charging along like troops in a battle,
All through the meadows the horses and cattle:
All of the sights of the hill and the plain
Fly as thick as driving rain;
And ever again, in the wink of an eye,
Painted stations whistle by.

Here is a child who clambers and scrambles,
All by himself and gathering brambles;
Here is a tramp who stands and gazes;
And there is the green for stringing the daisies!

Here is a cart run away in the road
Lumping along with man and load;
And here is a mill and there is a river:
Each a glimpse and gone for ever!

Robert Louis Stevenson

SEEING ALL MY FAMILY

Seeing all my family
together
at special occasions
is a brilliant firework show
going off.

Grandma is a sparkler,
Grandad is golden rain
making us brighter.
My cousins
are Catherine Wheels.
My dad is a banger
because he always talks too loud.
The best one of all
that lights up the sky
so everyone stares
is my mum
the incredible blast of sparkle
the rocket.

Every time we meet,
It always has the same effect
our family firework show.

Claire Salama (Aged 10)

WEASELS

He should have been at school
but instead, he was in bed,
his room more cheerful, brighter,
sheets and pillows whiter
than they'd ever been before.

Comics, bread with crusts cut off,
a jug of homemade lemonade,
Mum's hand so cool against his brow.
Now he had her to himself at last
he'd never want to go to school again.

And all because of little spots,
he raised his vest and thanked them.
Crimson pinpricks on his chest
- some clustered, some quite lonely -
like baby strawberries or beetroot.

Dr. Croker joked and felt his muscles.
'Superman! You'll soon be right as rain.'
But his voice from down the stairs
was stern and rather solemn
- and Mummy's sounded scared.

He strained to hear the words,
but they were speaking low. He slipped
out of bed, tiptoed to the door,
pressed his ear against the floor.
'Weasels. He's got weasels, I'm afraid.'

Weasels! He lay in bed and trembled.
Weasels. Furry-grey with pointed teeth.
They must have crept in as he slept,
gnawed and nibbled through the night.
He wondered how much of him was left.

His foot itched. Was it a hidden weasel?
Ankle, knee. Lots of them were there!
He screamed and she came flying.
Her arms were safe as blankets.
He didn't want to stop crying for a while.

John Latham

ANGRY

I shout,
I stamp,
I bounce around,
I stamp up the stairs,
I bounce on my bed,
Then my sister tries to calm me back down
So then I go outside where the trees are rattling
Then I feel it is a world of badness.
Then I go in the house and say I am sorry.

Donna Fisher (Aged 7)

LISTN BIG BRODDA DREAD, NA!

My sista is younga than me.
My sista outsmart five-foot three.
My sista is own car repairer
and yu nah catch me doing judo with her.

   I sey I wohn get a complex.
   I wohn get a complex.
   Then I see the muscles my sista flex.

My sista is tops at disco dance.
My sista is well into self-reliance.
My sista plays guitar and drums
and wahn see her knock back double rums.

   I sey I wohn get a complex.
   I wohn get a complex.
   Then I see the muscles my sista flex.

My sista doesn mind smears of grease and dirt.
My sista'll reduce yu with sheer muscle hurt.
My sista says no guy goin keep her phone-bound -
with own car mi sista is a wheel-hound.

   I sey I wohn get a complex.
   I wohn get a complex.
   Then I see the muscles my sista flex.

James Berry

I REMEMBER MY DAD

I remember his shouts when he was still at home.
I remember the day we rushed him in to hospital.
I remember trying to talk to him when he was in a coma.

He was my dad,
I remember him, I remember him.

I remember his blue eyes,
I remember his pale brown hair,
I remember his dark clear voice.

He was my dad,
I remember him, I remember him.

I remember his room 'Intensive care',
I was not allowed to see him,
Me and Mum were on our own.

He was my dad,
I remember him, I remember him.

I remember on the Saturday,
I had slept at my Nana's house,
My mum had gone to see him,
(She had brought some bad news).

He was my dad,
I remember him, I remember him.

Mum had some news,
Mum told me and I cried.
Everybody but Mum cried.
She had no tears left in her.

Louise Victoria Voce (Aged 9)

HANDS

Hands can pick things up like pencils
Hands can be kind and helpful
Hands wave at people you know
Hands clap when you listen to music
Hands help you eat and drink when it's tea time
Hands can push people when they be unkind
Hands are so helpful when you use them
Hands are beautiful.

Tamsyn Sear (Aged 7)

THERE ARE FOUR CHAIRS ROUND THE TABLE

There are four chairs round the table,
Where we sit down for our tea.
But now we only set places
For Mum, for Terry and me.

We don't chatter any more
About what we did in the day.
Terry and I eat quickly,
Then we both go out to play.

Mum doesn't smile like she used to.
Often, she just sits and sighs.
Sometimes, I know from the smudges,
That while we are out she cries.

John Foster

FIRSTS

First tinkling laugh,
First wailing cry,
First nagging doubt,
First shameful lie.

First day of school,
First tiny tooth,
First pangs of guilt,
First painful truth.

First white winter morning,
First fresh apple bite,
First star in the sky
On a cool, clear night.

First independence,
First leaving Mum,
First memories,
Firsts still to come.

Zoe Gardner

THE WRONG SIDE

My mother used to tell me
I'd got out of bed
on the wrong side, which was strange
as there was only one side
I could tumble from.
The other was hard against the wall
and all I did was crack
my knee, but still she insisted
that she was right, so one bright
morning I tried it out, squeezed
between the wall and my bed
then said nothing. She never knew.
I was puzzled.
My mother said how she'd teach me
to choose between wrong and right,
but if I got out of the right side
and that was wrong,
then who was right?

Brian Moses

TEA WITH AUNTY MABEL

If you ever go to tea with my Aunty Mabel,
Never put your elbows on the dining-room table,
Always wipe your shoes if you've been in the garden,
Don't ever burp. If you do, say pardon.
Don't put your feet on the new settee,
If she offers you a sugar lump, don't take three.

Don't dunk your biscuits, don't make crumbs,
Don't bite nails and don't suck thumbs.
Don't rock the budgie, don't tease the peke,
Speak when you're spoken to or else don't speak.
Do as you're told·and if you're not able,
Don't go to tea with my Aunty Mabel.

Jeanne Willis

MY AUNTIE

My auntie who lives in Llanfairpwllgwyngyllgogerych-
    wyrndrobwllllantysiliogogogoch
Has asked me to stay.

But unfortunately
Llanfairpwllgwyngyllgogerych-
    wyrndrobwllllantysiliogogogoch
Is a long, long way away.

Will I ever go to
Llanfairpwllgwyngyllgogerych-
    wyrndrobwllllantysiliogogogoch?
It's difficult to say.

Colin West

MY GRANNY IS A SUMO WRESTLER

My granny is six foot three
My granny is built like a tree
My granny says - Nothing
I mean nothing
Frightens me.

When Granny walks down the streets
She scares every man she meets
Nobody gonna mess with her
My granny is a Sumo Wrestler.

My granny is six foot three
My granny she's built like a tree
My granny says - Nothing
I mean nothing
Frightens me.

My granny does what she likes
My granny rides two motor bikes (at the same time)
My granny she breaks down doors
My granny bends bars with her jaws.

My granny she's six foot three (that's sitting down)
My granny she's built like a tree
My granny says - Nothing
Absolutely nothing
Frightens me.

My granny is a railway ganger
My granny is a wild head banger
My granny eats uncooked bison

My granny beat up Mike Tyson (in the first round).

My granny she's six foot three
My granny she's built like a tree (oak tree)
My granny says - Nothing
And I mean nothing
Ever
   Ever
      Ever
         Frightens me.

Gareth Owen

WHEN I AM OLD

When I am old, don't expect me to like it.
No big comfy cardigans for me.
No sensible shoes and no wrinkled stockings.

When I am old, I won't do crosswords.
No knitting needles that click and clack.
No shawls down my bent old back.

When I am old, I shall have a cat,
to keep me company
to sit with me on my lap.

When I am old, don't expect me to enjoy it.
I'll get a horrible cough,
and see the doctor every day.

When I am old and my legs won't work
and my shoulders feel sore,
I hope that someone will come to my door.

When I am old I'll take my teeth out at night,
And hang my wig on the chair,
And then I'll dream that I'm young again.

Amelia Clarke (Aged 12)

THE 'SLEEPING-BAG'

On the outside grows the furside, on the inside grows the skinside.
So the furside is the outside, and the skinside is in the inside.
As the skinside is the inside, and the furside is the outside;
One 'side' likes the skinside inside, and the furside on the outside.
Others like the skinside outside, and the furside on the inside;
As the skinside is the hardside, and the furside is the soft side.
If you turn the skinside outside, thinking you will side with that 'side',
Then the soft side, furside's inside, which some argue is the wrong side.
If you turn the furside outside, as you say it grows on that side;
Then your outside's next the skinside, which for comfort's not the right side:
For the skinside is the cold side, and your outside's not your warm side;
And two cold sides coming side by side are not right sides one 'side' decides.
If you decide to side with that 'side,' turn the outside, furside, inside:
Then the hard side, cold side, skinside's, beyond all question, inside outside.

Herbert George Ponting

NIGHT LIGHTS

There is no need to light a night-light
On a light night like tonight;
For a night-light's light's a slight light
When the moonlight's white and bright.

Anonymous

NIGHT RIDE

When I can't sleep
I shut my door
And sit on the rug
On my bedroom floor.

I open the window.
I close my eyes
And say magic words
Till my carpet flies.

Zooming over gardens,
Chasing after bats,
Hooting like an owl
And frightening the cats.

Then when I feel sleepy
And dreams are in my head,
I fly back through my window
And snuggle down in bed.

Celia Warren

GRANDPA BEAR'S LULLABY

The night is long
But fur is deep.
You will be warm
In winter sleep.

The food is gone
But dreams are sweet
And they will be
Your winter meat.

The cave is dark
But dreams are bright
And they will serve
As winter light.

Sleep, my little cubs, sleep.

Jane Yolen

HOW FAR ?

'How far away
Is the evening star?'
'Ask the night horse.
He knows how far.

Talk to him gently.
Give him honey and hay
And seven bells for his bridle
And he will take you away.

Snorting white fire
He will stream through the air
Past mountains of the moon
And the rainbow's stair.

And if you go singing
Through the dark and the cold
Your purse will be filled
With silver and gold.'

Olive Dove

WHEN I CLOSE MY EYES

When I close my eyes at night,
Lying in my bed,
My pillow fills with stories.
Legends fill my head.

Stories of mighty kings
And giants running tall,
Legends of fierce monsters
And fairies very small.

Stories from China,
Where dragons never die,
And legends from India
Where elephants can fly.

When I close my eyes at night,
Lying in my bed,
My pillow fills with stories.
Legends fill my head.

Andrew Collett

AUTHOR INDEX

John Agard
The Speller's Bag 83
Joan Aiken
How to Make a Sailor's
Pie 126
Finola Akister
St. George and the Dragon 90
Jez Alborough
Underwater, Holding Nose 29
Moira Andrew
Sleeping Cats 100
Anonymous
A Trip to Morrow 135
Hints on Pronunciation 50
I Asked the Little Boy Who
Cannot See 62
I Had A Nickel 38
If You Should Meet a
Crocodile 116
Imagine 92
Jamaican Clap Rhyme 55
'Mummy, Oh Mummy' 128
Night Lights 151
One Old Ox 58
Queen Nerfertiti 82
Ten Fat Sausages 40
That Sinking Feeling 123
The Biggest Firework 17
The Cats of Kilkenny 101
The Frog 107
The Relentless Pursuit of the
12-Toed Snortiblog! 96
The Surprising Number 37 58
The Young Bard of Japan 50
Thumping, Stumping,
Bumping, Jumping 49
Twelve Huntsmen 61
Two Times Table 59
Terry Baylis
Jealousy 69
James Berry
Listn Big Brodda Dread,
Na! 142
Keith Bosley
Guardian 99
Nicola Brophy
If I Moved House! 26

Palmer Brown
The Spangled
Pandemonium 94
Barry Buckingham
My Bargain Bag of
Question Marks 48
The Witch and the AA Man 80
Thomas Campbell
The Parrot 118
Charles E. Carryl
The Sleepy Giant 84
Remy Charlip
Two Octopuses Got
Married 119
Amelia Clarke
When I Am Old 150
Sara Coleridge
The Months 10
Andrew Collett
When I Close My Eyes 155
Stanley Cook
Chips 38
The Pocket Calculator 44
Pie Corbett
Wind Poem 18
Sue Cowling
Today, in Strong Colours 65
Lucy Davis
'Are We Nearly
There Yet?' 136
Tomie de Paola
The Secret Place 68
Peter Dixon
I'd Like to be a Teabag 36
Berlie Doherty
Mushrooms 37
Olive Dove
How Far? 154
Lord Alfred Douglas
The Hen 108
Richard Edwards
If Only I Could Drive a
Train 137
Ralph Waldo Emerson
Fable 114
Gavin Ewart
The Weather 11

Eric Finney
Mystery Story 45
Whoppers 86
Donna Fisher
Angry 141
Robert Fisher
My New Year's
Resolutions 9
John Foster
There are Four Chairs
Round the Table 144
Zoe Gardner
Firsts 145
Pamela Gillilan
First Fox 113
Nigel Gray
My Cat 102
Philip C. Gross
Walls I Scream 72
Sarah Gunn
Washing Up 28
Gregory Harrison
The Heron 109
Michael Harrison
Wanted 89
Matthew Hinton
Kitchen Noises 47
Russell Hoban
Old Man Ocean 126
Geoffrey Holloway
Blue Tits 107
Kevin Horton
Who Will Go First? 120
Patricia Hubbell
Concrete Mixers 20
Ted Hughes
Roger the Dog 104
Elizabeth Jennings
The Secret Brother 66
Mike Jubb
The Pyramids 116
Jean Kenward
The Monster 124
Ian Larmont
Overtaking 136
Wendy Larmont
Chinese New Year 12

John Latham
Weasels 140
Edward Lear
The Quangle Wangle's Hat 97
Marian Lines
Looking Down on Roofs 24
Jean Little
Pearls 69
Daphne Lister
Snow Clouds 19
Aaron Lockwood
Hair 54
Henry Wadsworth Longfellow
Rain in Summer 16
Wes Magee
The Electronic House 26
Katherine Mansfield
Little Brother's Secret 66
F.R McCreary
The Fog 18
Roger McGough
The Sound Collector 30
Colin McNaughton
At Long Last, Spring Has Arrived! 13
May Britton Miller
Camel 115
Spike Milligan
Goliath 127
Tony Mitton
Music 52
Pat Moon
Opening a Packet of Biscuits 39
Tiger in a Zoo 129
Brian Morse
A Lesson 34
Brian Moses
The Wrong Side 146
Grace Nichols
Break Dance 46
I Like 76
Mango 33
Sea Timeless Song 125
Riad Nourallah
An Alphabet for the Planet 130
Mary O'Neill
What is Black? 62
Gareth Owen
Life as a Sheep 110

Out in the City 21
My Granny is a Sumo Wrestler 148
Real Life 133
Unemployable 87
Bital Patel
Summer Days 15
Brian Patten
Burying the Dog in the Garden 105
I've Never Heard the Queen Sneeze 88
Herbert George Ponting
'The Sleeping-Bag' 151
Joan Poulson
Graffiti 22
Voice in the Night 74
William Brighty Rands
The Dream of a Boy who Lived at Nine Elms 60
Irene Rawnsley
Fisherman's Tale 91
Time to Dust the Daffodils 14
Treasure Trove 70
Alastair Reid
A Spell for Sleeping 84
James Reeves
Queer Things 93
Daniel Ribenfors
Learning to Read 51
E. V. Rieu
The Paint Box 64
Theodore Roethke
The Bat 114
Christina Rossetti
Coral 122
What is Pink? 64
When Fishes Set Umberllas Up 96
Claire Salama
Seeing All My Family 139
R. C. Scriven
The Marrog 41
Tamsin Sear
Hands 144
Chief Seattle
How Can One Sell the Air? 132
Danielle Sensier
Breakfast 34
Ian Serraillier
Anne and the Field-Mouse 112

The Witch's Cat 77
Pauline Stewart
Goodbye Granny 134
Robert Louis Stevenson
From a Railway Carriage 138
Windy Nights 16
William Makepeace Thackeray
A Tragic Story 95
Colin Thiele
Bumblefoot 103
Judith Thurman
Mare 106
Nick Toczek
The Dragon Who Ate Our School 42
Traditional
The Hairy Toe 78
The Wraggle Taggle Gipsies 24
Traditional Inuit Song
Spring Fjord 121
Steve Turner
It's Raining Cats and Dogs 87
Words I Like 53
Louise Victoria Voce
I Remember My Dad 143
Michelle Walker
The Walk 127
Celia Warren
Night Ride 152
Colin West
Chameleons 120
Geraldine Giraffe 117
My Auntie 147
Socks 56
Jeanne Willis
Tea With Aunty Mabel 146
Katie Wilson
Knees 55
Raymond Wilson
The Lighthouse 122
William Wordsworth
A Change in the Year 13
Kit Wright
Give Up Slimming, Mum 32
Jane Yolen
Grandpa Bear's Lullaby 153
Peter Young
Hands 54

ACKNOWLEDGEMENTS

John Agard: 'The Speller's Bag'. By kind permission of John Agard c/o Caroline Sheldon Literary Agency from *Grandfather's Old Bruk-a-down Car* published by Bodley Head 1994. **Terry Baylis:** ' Jealousy'. From *Wondercrump 3* edited by Jennifer Curry. By permission of Random House. **James Berry:** 'Listn Big Brodda Dread, Na!' from *When I Dance*, Hamish Hamilton 1988. Repeinted by permission of The Peters Fraser and Dunlop Group Limited on behalf of James Berry. **Keith Bosley:** 'Guardian'. By permission of Keith Bosley. **Nicola Brophy:** 'If I Moved House'. From *Wondercrump 1* edited by Jennifer Curry. By permission of Random House. **Palmer Brown:** 'The Spangled Pandemonium'. By permission of Faber and Faber. **Barry Buckingham:** 'My Bargain Bag of Question Marks', 'The Witch and the AA Man'. By permission of Barry Buckingham. **Amelia Clarke:** 'When I am Old'. From *Wondercrump 3* edited by Jennifer Curry. By permission of Random House. **Elizabeth J Coatsworth:** 'On a Night of Snow'. By permission of Catherine B Barnes from *Night and the Cat* published by Macmillan NY 1950. **Andrew Collett:** 'When I Close My Eyes'. By permission of Andrew Collett. **Stanley Cook:** 'Chips', 'The Pocket Calculator'. © the estate of Stanley Cook. **Pie Corbett:** 'Wind Poem'. By permission of Pie Corbett. **Sue Cowling:** 'Today, in strong colours'. By permission of Sue Cowling. **Lucie Davis:** 'Are We Nearly There Yet?'. From *Wondercrump 1* edited by Jennifer Curry. By permission of Random House. **Berlie Doherty:** 'Mushrooms'. By permission of Berlie Doherty. **Eric Finney:** 'Mystery Story', 'Whoppers'. By permission of Eric Finney. **Donna Fisher:** 'Angry'. From *Wondercrump 1* edited by Jennifer Curry. By permission of Random House. **Robert Fisher:** 'My New Year's Resolutions'. By permission of Robert Fisher. **John Foster:** 'There are four chairs round the table'. First published in *A Fifth Poetry Book* compiled by John Foster (Oxford University Press) included by permission of the author. **Pamela Gillilan:** ' First Fox'. By permission of Pamela Gillilan. **Nigel Gray:** 'My Cat' by Nigel Gray from *Another First Poetry Book* (Oxford University Press, 1987) © Nigel Gray 1998. **Philip C Gross:** 'Walls I Scream'. By permission of Philip C Gross. **Sarah Gunn:** 'Washing Up'. From *Wondercrump 3* edited by Jennifer Curry. By permission of Random House. **Gregory Harrison:** 'The Heron'. © Gregory Harrison. First published by Oxford University Press 1968 in *Posting Letters*, reprinted by permission of the author. **Michael Harrison:** 'Wanted'. By permission of Michael Harrison. **Matthew Hinton:** 'Kitchen Noises'. From *Wondercrump 1* edited by Jennifer Curry. By permission of Random House. **Russell Hoban:** 'Old Man Ocean'. By permission of Russell Hoban & Heinemann from *The Pedalling Man*. **Geoffrey Holloway:** 'Blue Tits'. By permission of Mrs Patricia Holloway. **Kevin Horton:** 'Who Will Go First?'. From *Wondercrump 1* edited by Jennifer Curry. By permission of Random House. **Ted Hughes:** 'Roger the Dog' by Ted Hughes from *What is the Truth*. Reprinted by permission of Faber and Faber. **Elizabeth Jennings:** 'The Secret Brother'. From *The Secret Brother*, Macmillan 1966. By permission of David Higham Associates. **Mike Jubb:** 'The pyramids'. By permission of Mike Jubb. **Jean Kenward:** ' The Monster'. By permission of Jean Kenward. **Wendy Larmont:** 'Chinese New Year'. By permission of Wendy Larmont. **Ian Larmont:** 'Overtaking'. By permission of Ian Larmont. **John Latham:** 'Weasels'. By permission of John Latham. **Marion Lines:** 'Looking down on Roofs'. From *Tower Blocks* by Marion Lines, first published in the UK by Orchard Books, a division of the Watts Publishing Group. **Jean Little:** 'Pearls' from *Hey World, Here I Am!* by Jean Little used by permission of Kids Can Press Ltd., Toronto. © by Jean Little. **Aaron Lockwood:** 'Hair'. From *Wondercrump 1* edited by Jennifer Curry. By permission of Random House. **Wes Magee:** 'The electronic house'. By permission of Wes Magee. **Roger McGough:** 'The Sound Collector'. Reprinted by permission of the Peters Fraser and Dunlop Group Limited on behalf of Roger McGough. **Colin McNaughton:** 'At Long Last, Spring Has Arrived!'. From *There's An Awful Lot of Weirdos in Our Neighbourhood* © 1987 Colin McNaughton. Reproduced by permission of the publisher Walker Books Ltd., London. **Spike Milligan:** 'Goliath'. By permission of Spike Milligan Productions Ltd. **Tony Mitton:** 'Music'. By permission of Tony Mitton. **Brian Morse:** 'A Lesson'. By permission of Rogers, Coleridge & White Ltd. **Brian Moses:** 'The Wrong Side'. By permission of Brian Moses. **Grace Nichols:** 'Mango', 'Sea timeless song'. By permission of the Virago Press from *Fat Black Woman's Poems* by Grace Nichols. 'Break Dance' by permission of the Virago Press from *Lazy Thoughts of a Lazy Woman* by Grace Nichols. **Riad Nourallah:** 'An Alphabet for the Planet'. By permission of Dr Riad Nourallah. **Mary O'Neill:** 'What is black?'. © 1960 by Curtis Publishing Company from *Hairstones and Halibut Bones* by Mary O'Neill and Leonard Weisgard, Ill. Used by permission of Doubleday, a division of Bantam Doubleday Dell Publishing Group, Inc. **Gareth Owen:** 'Out in the City', 'Unemployable', 'Life as a Sheep', Real Life', 'My Granny is a Sumo Wrestler'. By permission of Rogers, Coleridge & White Ltd. **Bital Patel:** 'Summer Days'. From *Wondercrump 1* edited by Jennifer Curry. By permission of Random House. **Brian Patten:** 'I've Never Heard the Queen Sneeze', 'Burying the Dog in the Garden'. Copyright © Brian Patten 1985. 'Embrionic Mega Stars'. Copyright © Brian Patten, 1985. Reproduced by permission of the author c/o Rogers, Coleridge & White Ltd. **Joan Poulson:** 'Graffiti', 'Voice in the Night'. Copyright © Joan Poulson. **Irene Rawnsley:** 'Time to Dust the Daffodils', 'Treasure Trove', 'Fisherman's Tale'. By permission of Reed Books. **James Reeves:** 'Queer Things'. © James Reeves from *Complete Poems for Children* (Heinemann). Reprinted by permission of the James Reeves Estate. **Daniel Ribenfors:** 'Learning to Read'. From *Wondercrump 2* edited by Jennifer Curry. By permission of Random House. **E V Rieu:** 'The Paint Box'. By permission of Penelope Rieu. **Theodore Roethke:** 'The Bat'. 'The Bat by Theodore Roethke from *Collected Poems*. Reprinted by permission of Faber and Faber. **Clare Salama:** 'Seeing All My Family'. From *Wondercrump 3* edited by Jennifer Curry. By permission of Random House. **R C Scriven:** 'The Marrog'. Reproduced by permission of The Agency (London) Ltd © R C Scriven 1975. **Tamsyn Sear:** 'Hands'. From *Wondercrump 2* edited by Jennifer Curry. By permission of Random House. **Danielle Sensier:** 'Breakfast'. By permission of Danielle Sensier. **Ian Serraillier:** 'The Witch's Cat', 'Anne and the Field Mouse'. By permission of Anne Serraillier. **Pauline Stewart:** 'Goodbye Granny'. By permission of Pauline Stewart & The Bodley Head from *Singing Down the Breadfruit*. **Nick Toczek:** 'The Dragon Who Ate Our School'. By permission of Nick Toczek. **Louise Victoria Voce:** 'I Remember My Dad'. From *Wondercrump 2* edited by Jennifer Curry. By permission of Random House. **Michelle Walker:** 'The Walk'. From *Wondercrump 1* edited by Jennifer Curry. By permission of Random House. **Celia Warren:** 'Night Ride'. By permission of Celia Warren. **Colin West:** 'Socks', 'Geraldine Giraffe', 'Chameleons', 'My Auntie'. By permission of Colin West. **Katie Wilson:** 'Knees'. From *Wondercrump 2* edited by Jennifer Curry. By permission of Random House. **Raymond Wilson:** 'The Lighthouse'. By permission of Mrs G M Wilson. **Kit Wright:** 'Give Up Slimming Mum'. By permission of Kit Wright. **Peter Young:** 'Hands'. By permission of Mrs Joyce Young.

Every effort has been made to trace copyright holders but in some cases this has not proved possible. The publisher will be happy to rectify any such errors or omissions in future reprints and/or new editions. In particular, we have been unable to contact the following: **Joan Aiken:** 'How to Make Sailors Pie'. **Finola Akister:** 'St George and the Dragon'. **Jez Alborough:** 'Underwater, holding nose'. **Moira Andrew:** 'Sleeping Cats'. **James Berry:** 'Listn Big Broda Dread, Na!'. **Remy Charlip:** 'Two Octopuses got married'. **Peter Dixon:** 'I'd like to be a Teabag'. **Olive Dove:** 'How Far?'. **Richard Edwards:** 'If Only I Could Drive a Train'. **Gavin Ewart:** 'The Weather'. **F R McCreary:** 'The Fog'. **Zoe Gardner:** 'Firsts'. **Patricia Hubbell:** 'Concrete Mixers'. **Daphne Lister:** 'Snow Clouds'. **Mary Britton Miller:** 'Camel'. **Pat Moon:** 'Opening a Packet of Biscuits', 'Tiger in a Zoo'. **Grace Nichols:** 'I Like'. **Tomie de Paola:** 'The Secret Place'. **Herbert George Ponting:** 'The Sleeping Bag'. **Alastair Reid:** 'A Spell for Sleeping'. **Colin Thiele:** 'Bumblefoot'. **Judith Thurman:** 'Mare'. **Steve Turner:** 'Words I Like', 'It's Raining Cats and Dogs'. **Jeanne Willis:** 'Tea with Aunty Mabel'. **Jane Yolen:** 'Grandpa Bear's Lullaby'.